Successful Recruitment

Successful Recruitment

How to Recruit the Right People For Your Business

Stephen Amos, MSc

BEP BUSINESS EXPERT PRESS

First published in 2020 by
Business Expert Press, LLC
222 East 46th Street, New York, NY 10017
www.businessexpertpress.com

ISBN-13: 978-1-94858-063-2 (paperback)
ISBN-13: 978-1-94858-064-9 (e-book)

Business Expert Press Human Resource Management and Organizational Behavior Collection

Collection ISSN: 1946-5637 (print)
Collection ISSN: 1946-5645 (electronic)

Cover image licensed by Ingram Image, StockPhotoSecrets.com

Cover and interior design by Exeter Premedia Services Private Ltd., Chennai, India

First edition: 2020

10 9 8 7 6 5 4 3 2 1

Printed in the United States of America.

Abstract

Successful Recruitment will provide the practical guidance and underpinning knowledge you need to recruit the right people for your business, and avoid the many pitfalls that can arise in the recruitment process. It begins by identifying why recruitment is so often unsuccessful, leading to time, money, and energy being wasted in recruiting people who lack the attributes required to succeed in your organization. It then sets out how you can put in place an effective recruitment process, by:

- Planning the process before you start.
- Laying firm foundations, by making sure that job descriptions, person specifications, and application forms are fit for purpose.
- Ensuring that your advertising is targeted to reach the right applicants.
- Sifting and shortlisting to ensure that the right candidates are selected for interview.
- Developing the knowledge, skills, and processes to ensure that interviews enable you to gather the information you need to make a robust assessment of each candidate's ability to do the job.
- Effectively utilizing other assessment methods alongside the interview.
- Concluding the process properly and ensuring that the right candidate is appointed.
- Ensuring that the appointed candidate is effectively inducted into your organization.

Successful Recruitment pays particular attention to the recruitment interview, explaining three different approaches to interviewing and the key skills required to conduct an effective interview.

Successful Recruitment also includes a chapter which considers some of the specific issues involved in recruiting internationally.

The book concludes by considering the future of recruitment, identifying trends and innovations which will affect how you recruit over the next decade.

Keywords

recruitment; sifting; shortlisting; interview; interviewing; behavior description interviewing; model answer based interviewing; strengths based interviewing; competency; competencies; assessment; assessing; rapport building; questions; questioning; listening; note taking; selection; selecting; record keeping

Contents

Introduction

Effective recruitment is critical to an organization's success. If there is any truth in that well-worn cliché that "people are an organization's greatest asset," then it would seem obvious that close attention should be paid to ensuring that:

- Recruitment processes are robust.
- Job descriptions and person specifications are clear and up to date.
- Selection criteria are clearly defined and understood.
- Panel members are trained in the knowledge and skills required to sift applications and interview candidates effectively.

As I said above, it would seem obvious ... but research into recruitment tells a different story.

In his 2004 article "Making Decisions" Peter Drucker observed that, although decisions around hiring and promoting people are among the most crucial and the most difficult of all decisions a leader will make, only one-third of such choices turn out to be truly successful, one-third are "effective draws" with the final third being a failure.

What are the reasons for this high level of failure? And has anything changed or improved since 2004?

Four Key Reasons for Ineffective Recruitment

The reasons for ineffective recruitment include:

- Lack of planning
- Focusing on the wrong criteria
- Poorly thought-out processes
- Inadequate training

- Lack of planning

In many cases no thought is given to the recruitment process until a vacancy arises. A key employee gives a month's notice, out of the blue. Suddenly the pressure is on to recruit a replacement. No time to check and update the job description! No time to write a person specification! No time to think about where to target our advertising! No time to create a selection process which will give you the best chance of finding the right candidate.

If recruitment is to be effective, you need to start thinking about it before you need to fill a vacancy. Think about the changing demands on your organization. Analyze job roles and update job descriptions and person specifications accordingly. Think about the type of people your business needs to attract, and where you will need to advertise in order to reach them. Think about the selection processes which will most effectively test candidates for the attributes you are looking for to ensure the continuing success of your business. In the words of Michael O'Leary, in his 2015 article "Why does Recruitment Fail?"

Drill the well before you're thirsty

- Focusing on the wrong criteria

We live in a rapidly changing world, where demands on employees are constantly evolving. If you fail to plan in advance for recruitment you are more likely to fall back on old, outdated job descriptions, which reflect how the job used to look, rather than how it looks now—let alone how it will look in the future. This leads to candidates being assessed against criteria which no longer reflect what the job requires, at each stage of the process. This may mean that candidates with potential might even get sifted out before the interview stage, so you don't even get the opportunity to meet them.

In their article "The Definitive Guide to Recruiting in Good Times and Bad," Claudio Fernández-Aráoz, Boris Groysberg, and Nitin Nohria report that, when making decisions on whom to hire, almost half of firms consider the number of years of relevant work experience to be a top reason to recruit a particular candidate. There are two significant problems with this. Firstly, length of experience tells you nothing about ability. The candidate may have spent years treading water, doing just enough to get by. Secondly, this type of backward-looking process does not tell you about a candidate's ability to adapt and change. Fernández-Aráoz, Groysberg, and Nohria were stunned to discover that, despite today's demand for organizational transformation and innovation, only 11 percent of recruiting organizations tested a candidate's ability to learn new things.

- Inadequate processes and systems

Often selection processes are not fit for purpose. Unstructured interviews give only a 50/50 chance of selecting the right candidate, and are prone to resulting in selection decisions which are influenced by the interviewers' unconscious biases. Structured interviews are more likely to produce evidence-based decisions, but these will only be reliable if the interviews are based on the right criteria in the first place. Using a wider range of methods, such as tests, exercises, and simulations, will enable you to develop a fuller picture of candidates' abilities—but require an investment of time and money. Given the costs of ineffective recruitment, which might result in you appointing an incompetent candidate who damages your business, I would suggest that this is an investment which is worth making.

Please do not think I am suggesting throwing money at the problem. Some organizations have spent huge sums of money in developing recruitment processes which are so complicated that both recruiters and applicants are baffled as to what is expected of them. Keep the processes as simple as possible, but make sure that they test the right things.

Sometimes organizations invest heavily in systems which fail to do an adequate job. One organization I know of persists in using a computerized sifting tool, despite everyone being frustrated that it persistently sifts out candidates that they would like to interview. Why do they persist with it? Because it cost a lot of money! If we are going to use technology in recruitment, we need to ensure that it works for us.

- Inadequate training

I am often surprised by organizations which spend large sums of money developing complex processes and systems for recruitment, but fail to invest in training people who have to operate these processes. Like most training, courses in interviewing skills have become shorter, with some aspects now delivered through e-learning. E-learning—like this book—will help you to develop your knowledge, but is no substitute for practicing your skills, in an environment where you can receive feedback from an experienced observer on what you have done well and where you need to improve.

For this reason I recommend seeking opportunities to conduct practice interviews, perhaps by interviewing a more junior colleague who wishes to develop their abilities as an interviewee. If possible involve a colleague who is a skilled, experienced interviewer, who can demonstrate the interviewing skills set out in this book, as well as providing you with feedback on your skills and your candidate with feedback on their performance. Finally, it is often enlightening to video these interviews, enabling you to see how you come across as an interviewer. Cell phones make it easy for us to do this.

How This Book Will Help You

If you are new to recruitment—this book will take you through a structured approach to each stage of the recruitment process, enabling you to understand and follow best practice.

If you already have experience in recruitment, this book will enable you to review your own practices and skills, and continue your professional development as a recruiter.

If you are a recruitment specialist, this book will help you to review the practices and procedures followed by you and your organization.

If you are about to experience the recruitment process as a candidate, this book will help you to understand the selection processes and what recruiters are looking for at each stage.

For anyone reading this book, its aim is to help you to understand and follow recruitment processes which will enable you to be successful in selecting the right candidates for your organization, who will do a great job for you once they have been appointed.

CHAPTER 1

Planning Recruitment

This chapter covers the importance of planning; including three approaches to interviewing: Behavior Description Interviewing, Model Answer-Based Interviewing, and Strengths-Based Interviewing. It also considers other assessment methods to use alongside the interview.

As I have highlighted in the Introduction, recruitment campaigns are often less successful than they should be. All too often organizations end up hiring the wrong person, for the wrong reasons, and end up spending time and money on managing a poor performer, instead of spending it on developing a talented new employee.

Like most things that go wrong, this is usually down to inadequate planning. All too often the plan for a recruitment campaign is presented as:

1. Write a job description
2. Advertise
3. Shortlist
4. Interview
5. Appoint

Looks simple, doesn't it? And for a busy executive, simple is tempting. But in reality, this superficial approach to planning recruitment leads to poor decisions being made, at each stage of the process, and ultimately the wrong people being hired.

To recruit effectively, we need to think deeply about each stage of the process. We also need to plan the process holistically, so that each stage flows naturally into the next. I've encountered organizations where no thought is given to how interviews are to be structured, and what questions are to be asked, until the day before they take place. The risk of this last minute planning is that we fall back on the approaches we have always used—even if evidence suggests they have not been effective!

The most common outcome of this is hiring candidates on the basis of their experience, because that is easy to test at interview, rather than their potential, which is much harder to test.

If interviews are to be effective, then we need to plan our approach to them right at the start of the recruitment campaign. We also need to recognize that an interview is not always the best way to test candidates' full range of abilities. Indeed, relying on evidence from interviews alone often leads to poor recruitment decisions, because panels are seduced by candidates who talk persuasively and present themselves well. Sometimes there is little substance behind these positive first impressions—something it would be useful to identify before making the appointment.

So we're going to start by considering three approaches you can take to conducting the interview, then identify the other selection methods you may wish to use alongside the interview. By planning ahead, and putting the right combination of processes in place, you give yourself the best chance of recruiting a candidate who will do a great job for your business.

Approaches to Interviewing

Three approaches to interviewing are:

- Behavior Description Interviewing
- Model Answer-Based Interviewing
- Strengths-Based Interviewing

Some organizations stick rigidly to one of these approaches, but over recent years it has become increasingly common to use a *blended* approach, combining these different approaches together in order to gain a full picture of the applicant's suitability for the job.

Behavior Description Interviewing

Behavior Description Interviewing is based on the principle that the best guide to how someone will behave in the future is how they have behaved in the past. It is also sometimes known as

Evidence-based interviewing—because it involves obtaining evidence of what people have done.

Or

Competency-based interviewing—because it is used to test the applicant's competence to do the job, often by asking questions derived from the organization's competency framework.

The job interview is sometimes described as having been "born" in 1921, when Thomas Edison developed a standardized list of questions to ask job applicants. The list of 150 questions included:

- Where do we import cork from?
- How is sulfuric acid made?
- Who was Hannibal?

The questions were designed to test applicants' levels of knowledge and education. While they are very different from the questions we would ask candidates today, the approach of asking the same set of questions to all applicants provided the origins of today's recruitment interview.

The following year business psychologist H. L. Hollingsworth studied the rankings given to candidates applying for positions in the army. Several officers interviewed the same applicants, but Hollingsworth's study revealed wide variations in their assessments. This was due to each interviewer adopting their own approach, with no consistency or standardization.

In response to such studies recruiters began adding more structure to interviews. Questions were drawn up in advance, so that each interviewer would ask the same set of questions to each interviewee. The results of this were greater consistency of approach and improved accuracy of results.

Job descriptions started to be used to clarify what successful applicants for a post would be required to do. One study revealed that managers assessing candidates against job descriptions were less likely to be influenced by irrelevant details, than managers assessing candidates in a less structured way.

In 1980 Latham, Saari, Pursell, and Campion developed the approach which became known as *critical incident* or *situational* interviewing. This involved describing a scenario to a candidate, then asking them questions

to identify how they would respond. Interviewers were also given instructions on how to rate the candidates' answers. Once again, this development
improved the consistency and accuracy (measured against subsequent job
performance) of results.

In 1982 Tom Janz took elements of this approach and developed
Behavior Description Interviewing. Whereas Situational Interviewing
asks candidates what they *would do* in a specific situation, Behavior
Description Interviewing asks candidates to describe what they *actually
did* in a specific situation. This meant that the answers given would
describe actual behavior, instead of being purely hypothetical. As with
previous developments, Janz found that using this approach increased
both consistency and accuracy of interviews in identifying suitable
candidates.

Subsequent studies suggest that Behavior Description Interviewing
is 66 to 70 percent successful in identifying candidates who will go on
to succeed in the job. Unstructured approaches only achieve around 46
percent success rate. The chances of maximizing the success of Behavior
Description Interviewing are increased if it is used intelligently alongside
the other approaches described in this chapter.

Model Answer-Based Interviewing

One of the criticisms of Behavior Description Interviewing is that, due
to its emphasis on past performance, it may not be effective in identifying candidates who have the potential to be successful, but have not yet
had sufficient opportunities to demonstrate this in practice. By operat-
ing Behavior Description Interviewing in a simplistic way, we run the
risk of treating young or inexperienced candidates unfairly, and possibly missing out on selecting candidates with the greatest long-term
potential.

One way of overcoming this is by using Model Answer-Based Interviewing alongside the Behavioral approach. If there are gaps in a candidate's experience it is therefore possible still to assess them, and to rate
their answers against those given by more experienced candidates.

Model Answer-Based Interviewing involves asking hypothetical
questions about situations that the candidate may have to deal with if

appointed. The interviewer begins by describing the context and relating the situation to the job, then asks the candidate to describe what they would do. For example:

> As you are aware, one of the key aspects of this job is managing the office budget. What would you do first if the Managing Director called you into her office and told you that you have to make immediate savings of 20 percent?
>
> As you are aware, one of the key aspects of this job is managing a team. What would you do if you came in one morning and found two team members having a stand-up row in the office?

Of course, when using this technique it is important to have a clear idea of the answer you are looking for, and to have follow-up questions in mind for probing the candidate's answer in detail. The "model answer" should usually meet the "STAR" criteria:

Situation—good candidates will demonstrate their understanding of the situation, for example, by recapping the key points, or by asking clarifying questions.

Task—this involves analyzing the situation and identifying what needs to be done.

Actions—what specific actions would be required to resolve the situation?

Results—clear identification of the outcome required in order to resolve the initial problem.

Please note that Model Answer-Based Interviewing should not be used as a substitute for asking the candidate about real-life examples. As research has shown, real-life examples will give you the best indication of the candidate's abilities. However, blending Model Answer-Based Interviewing with Behavior Description Interviewing will enable you to ask about situations where the candidate has little or no experience, and gain a broader view of the candidate's talents and abilities.

Table 1.1 shows the pros and cons of the Behavior Description and Model Answer-Based approaches.

Table 1.1 Comparison of behavior description interviewing and model answer-based interviewing

	Behavior Description Interviewing	Model Answer-Based Interviewing
Pros	Quality evidence through real-life examples Through the use of probing questions interviewers should be able to test candidates' abilities in detail	Enables you to test candidates who may not have had sufficient "real-life" opportunities to demonstrate the criteria
Cons	Candidates may not give full and accurate accounts of what actually happened Examples on candidates' application forms may not be representative of their normal, day-to-day performance	Answers may not be representative of what the candidate would actually do in practice Easy to prepare "the perfect answer"—particularly if the questions are predict-able ones

Strengths-Based Interviewing

Strengths-based questions enable you to find out what a candidate is good at, and whether what they perceive as their strengths are a good fit with the strengths that need to be demonstrated in the job you have to fill, and more widely, in your organization.

There are three elements that determine whether something is a strength:

- *Performance*: the ability to perform an activity or demonstrate a behavior to a high level of capability or proficiency.
- *Engagement*: the candidate demonstrates that they feel moti-vated, enthused, and empowered when demonstrating the behavior or carrying out the activity.
- *Use*: the extent to which the candidate has regularly carried out the activity or demonstrated the behavior.

Strengths-based questions are a great way to start an interview. Most people feel comfortable talking about their strengths, so it enables the candidate to get the interview off to a good start by talking enthusiasti-cally about something they do well. By showing signs of encouragement while they are doing this, such as smiling and nodding, you will be able to build rapport with the candidate. Seeing how they respond to a question which enables the candidate to talk easily about their strengths also establishes a baseline for monitoring their demeanor during the rest of the interview. What questions lead them to appear less enthusiastic and motivated? Are these the areas where they are less confident in their abilities? And, if so, is this matched by the content of their answers?

There are two ways in which you can ask strengths-based questions. The first approach relates to *the candidate's strengths*. These questions might be very broad, for example:

Let's start the interview by getting you to tell us about the main strengths you think you can bring to this role.

A variation on this approach is to base the question on information provided by the candidate on their application form:

I see from your application form that you feel one of your strengths is your ability to motivate people. Tell me more about that.

The second approach to asking strengths-based questions is to relate them to the *strengths required in the role they have applied for*. For example:

We're looking for a candidate who has a real strength in quickly building great relationships with customers. Tell me how you do that.

It would be unwise to base a whole interview solely on strengths-based questions. One of the advantages of strengths-based questions is that they put the candidate at ease at the start of the interview, but using them throughout might make the interview too comfortable for the candidate, and may not enable you to test their ability to handle situations which take them out of their comfort zone. For this reason it is important to use a blended approach, using Strengths-Based Interviewing alongside Behavior Description Interviewing and Model Answer-Based Interviewing.

Other Assessment Methods

As I have already stated, there are many other assessment methods that can be used alongside the interview. Just as a blended approach enables you to obtain a full picture of the candidate's abilities at interview, using the right blend of assessment methods will enable you to gather evidence of the candidate's abilities from a range of different sources. These methods include:

- Video interviews
- Presentations
- Exercises
- Tests

Video interviews may be used as an alternative to face-to-face interviews, particularly if long distance travel would otherwise be required. They can also be used at the Sifting stage, to decide which candidates should be invited to a full face-to-face interview.

Presentations can easily be arranged alongside interviews. A short presentation will enable you to identify whether a candidate has the required skills for a position in an area such as training or sales.

A range of both *individual and group exercises* can be used to observe candidates carrying out activities in practice. Close observation will provide you with a great deal of information about their knowledge, skills, and attributes.

A wide range of *tests* are available and can provide valuable insights as long as you pay attention to selecting the right one and ensure that it is properly administered.

All of these methods can add value to your selection process. The key aspects to ensuring that they do are to:

1. Plan ahead, by identifying the information you will need to make your selection decision, then choosing the right combination of approaches to enable you to gather this information.
2. Take a holistic approach to selection, ensuring that the methods you use are compatible with one another, and appropriate to the nature of the role and the values of your organization.

3. Follow a *blended approach*, which will enable you to develop the fullest picture of candidates' abilities, and select the one who is best suited to the job.

The pros and cons of using these methods alongside the interview are discussed in Chapter 9.

Summary of Chapter 1—Planning Recruitment

In this chapter I have discussed the importance of considering a range of approaches when planning your recruitment process. This includes three approaches to interviewing:

Behavior Description Interviewing—based on the principle that the best guide to future performance is past performance. It therefore involves asking questions based on the candidate's experiences, such as, "What did you do ..." or "Tell us about a time when you ..."

Model Answer-Based Interviewing recognizes that not every candidate will have had experience of the range of situations you wish to ask about. It involves asking hypothetical questions, such as "What would you do ..." Candidates' answers are then assessed against model answers prepared in advance.

Strengths-Based Interviewing, which provides the candidate with the opportunity to talk about their strengths, and for you to test if these are aligned with the strengths required in the post they have applied for.

Planning a blended interview structure will enable you to utilize the benefits of each of these approaches to interviewing.

You may also wish to consider other assessment methods to use alongside the interview. These include:

- Video interviews
- Presentations
- Exercises
- Tests

Planning a recruitment process which utilizes a combination of these methods will enable you to gain a fuller picture of candidates' abilities, and make more reliable decisions about who should be appointed.

CHAPTER 2

Laying the Foundations

This chapter covers the job description, the person specification, candidate application forms, panel member rating form, and panel rating form.

The purpose of the recruitment process is to select the right candidate for the job. Often we focus our attention on the latter stages of the process—the interview and other forms of assessment—but in order to make sure these are effective we need to put in place firm foundations. This involves ensuring that:

- Everyone is clear about the requirements of the job.
- Applicants have the opportunity to provide relevant evidence of their ability to do the job.
- Panel members have an opportunity to systematically consider the evidence presented by applicants.

If this is to be achieved the following documents need to be produced:

- Job description
- Person specification
- Candidate application form
- Rating forms

Let's take a look at each of these in turn.

The Job Description

The job description defines the purpose of the job, its context within the organization, and its key tasks and accountabilities.

Job descriptions should be fairly brief and to the point. If a job description is too long it may be difficult for both applicants and panel members to identify the key aspects. There is also the risk of an overly detailed job description becoming restrictive—the applicant may get the impression that it encompasses everything that the job will ever entail. In changing times it is important for both applicants and panel members to understand that the job description is simply a snapshot of how the job looks at the current time.

For this reason it is unwise to simply send out the last job description that you had on file, which is the temptation when you feel under pressure and short of time. Make sure that the job description you use not only reflects how the job looks now, but also reflects how you will want it to look when the new job holder has been recruited.

If you work in a large organization you may need to check with HR before amending existing job descriptions—the changes you wish to make may have an effect on the grading of a job, which would have implications for the wider grading structure and the salary to be paid.

Following is an example of job description.

Example: Job Description

Job Title: Customer Service Manager
Grade: Executive Level
Salary Band: $xxxxx to $xxxxx
This post is based: Denver, Colorado
Reports to: Director of Customer Services
Budgetary Responsibility: $xxxxx
Staff Charge: xx customer service agents

Job Purpose

To plan, coordinate, and control the activities of the customer service team in order to maintain and enhance customer relationships and meet organizational and operational objectives.

Key Responsibilities

- Day-to-day management of customer services team, including monitoring of performance against sales targets, performance standards, and key competencies.
- Induction, training, and development of team members to continually improve product knowledge and service standards.
- Development and implementation of customer service policies, procedures, and service standards.
- Maintaining regular contact with customers to ensure customer satisfaction is maintained and any complaints are resolved promptly.
- Monitoring and analyzing customer service data with a view to maximizing customer satisfaction and profitability.
- Financial management: forecasting and managing delegated budget with a view to finding savings and reducing costs where possible.
- Work with Director of Customer Services to support and implement growth strategies.
- Coordinate and manage customer service projects and initiatives.

The Person Specification

Having prepared an up-to-date job description, your next task is to write a person specification.

While the job description is *task focused*, the person specification is *person focused*. It sets out the attributes, skills, knowledge, experience, and qualifications which are required in order to successfully carry out the tasks detailed in the job description. It breaks these requirements down into understandable and manageable chunks, enabling them to be clearly understood, and tested during the selection process.

The person specification should clearly differentiate between *Essential* and *Desirable* criteria for doing the job.

The *Essential* elements of the person specification are the "must have" requirements, without which it would not be possible to do the job effectively. These may include:

Qualifications, which demonstrate that the candidate has been educated to the required level. These may be *general* qualifications, which indicate that the candidate has achieved basic knowledge and skills requirements in areas such as literacy and numeracy; or *specific* qualifications, which demonstrate the candidate's knowledge and understanding in areas that are specifically relevant to the job.

Knowledge to do the job effectively. For example, if the job includes responsibilities relating to health and safety, it is important to ensure that the successful candidate has relevant knowledge of relevant health and safety regulations. In some cases achievement of a relevant qualification may be seen as evidence that the candidate has the required knowledge. However, it is important to bear in mind the following points:

1. Legislation and best practice requirements are subject to change. Achieving a qualification demonstrates that the candidate had the relevant knowledge and understanding at that time, but you will need to satisfy yourself that the candidate has kept up to date with changes since gaining their qualification.

2. Some candidates will have relevant knowledge but may not have obtained the qualifications which demonstrate this. In some instances you may decide that the qualification itself is essential, for example, if you are recruiting for a Corporate Finance Officer, you may specify an accountancy qualification as an essential requirement. In other roles, however, it may be possible for a candidate to demonstrate that they have the relevant knowledge to perform the role effectively, even if they have not acquired the relevant qualification. You may need to ask yourself which is likely to be the better candidate for the role:

Candidate A—who has an impressive-looking qualification, but little experience of applying their knowledge in practice;

Or

Candidate B—who does not have a qualification, but has built up their knowledge over many years of relevant work experience.

Experience of relevant work. If the successful candidate will immediately be taking up a position of responsibility, it may be essential that they can demonstrate relevant experience of applying their knowledge, skills, and attributes in a similar role. If you are recruiting for a trainee or apprentice, however, then experience will be less important than the candidate being able to demonstrate that they have the long-term potential to carry out the role effectively. So when considering whether experience is part of your essential criteria, you will need to decide whether you will need the successful candidate to perform effectively in the role as soon as they are appointed, or whether you are recruiting for the long term, with a period of training and development on the job before they are expected to become fully effective.

Competencies that are essential to effective performance in the role. Klemp (1980) defines a job competency as

> an underlying characteristic of a person which results in effective and/or superior performance in a job

By defining the essential competencies for the job, then testing candidates against them, we should be able to identify those candidates who will display effective or superior performance if appointed.

One of the ways in which this can be done is by breaking the competency down into specific behaviors which can be evidenced during the recruitment process. For example, a competency such as "Communicates effectively with others" may be evidenced through behaviors such as:

- Presents influentially to a wide range of people.
- Listens well and encourages two-way communication.
- Ensures that communication is understood through use of questioning and clarifying skills.

You may work in an organization that already has a clearly defined competency framework, and be familiar with using it when appraising staff performance or identifying training needs. If your business does not already have a competency framework, then you may find it helpful to develop one, as it provides a helpful foundation for a range of HR processes including recruitment and performance appraisal.

Once the relevant behaviors have been defined, they can be tested through:

The application form—by asking candidates to provide specific written examples of times when they have demonstrated the required behaviors.

The interview—by asking candidates questions about the times when they have demonstrated these behaviors, and probing these examples in detail.

Assessment center activities—where candidates are asked to carry out relevant tasks or activities, either individually or as part of a group, which provide an opportunity for them to demonstrate the required behaviors in practice.

While the *Essential* criteria are the "must have" requirements for the job, the *Desirable* criteria may be defined as the "nice to have" requirements. They may be factors that will enable the successful candidate to hit the ground running when they take up the role, but can be addressed through effective induction and training if they are not already in place. They may include:

- Experience/knowledge of IT/software already being used by the company.
- Experience of working in a similar organization.
- Experience/understanding of a specific client group.

These are desirable attributes, and if they are in place they will enable the selected candidate to become effective in the role more quickly. However, they are not essential, because if they are not already in place they can be developed by the successful candidate once appointed. For this reason, it is often more important for the successful candidate to have underlying characteristics such as adaptability and a desire to learn, than it is for them to have specific experience.

The benefit of specifying desirable criteria alongside essential criteria is that if you find yourself having to choose between a number of highly qualified candidates, all of whom have demonstrated the essential criteria for the role, you can then turn to the desirable criteria in order to decide which candidate is going to do the best job for you.

It is important that the recruitment process is fully transparent, and that candidates are informed of how their applications will be assessed. This enables them to provide relevant information and evidence, which in turn helps the panel to make their decisions. By documenting how they have assessed the candidates' evidence against the requirements of the person specification, panel members are also protected against any suggestions that the process has not been conducted fairly.

Following is an example of a person specification for the post of Customer Services Manager.

Example: Person specification

Criteria	Essential	Desirable	How assessed
Knowledge			
Good knowledge of Quality Management systems such as ISO 9000	√		Application form
Understands Health and Safety regulations and their application in a customer-facing environment	√		Interview
Working knowledge of MS Excel, MS Word, MS Outlook, and MS PowerPoint	√		Tests
Qualifications			Documents to be provided
Membership of a relevant professional body—for example, Institute of Customer Service		√	
Full clean driving license	√		
Experience			
Successful experience of working and managing people in a busy customer-facing environment	√		Application form
Has worked in a sales environment	√		Interview

	√		
Has had to manage and work within budgets	√		References
Has recruited people		√	
Competencies *Developing Customer Relations*	√		Application form
Attracts new customers by promoting products and services	√		Interview
Builds and maintains effective relationships with customers	√		References
Ensures team members provide a consistently high standard of customer service	√		
Promptly resolves problems for customers if things go wrong	√		
Communicating Effectively	√		
Presents influentially to a wide range of people			
Listens well and encourages two-way communication	√		
Ensures that communication is understood through use of questioning and clarifying skills	√		
Managing People	√		
Motivates team members to achieve and maintain high levels of performance	√		
Tackles poor performance promptly and effectively	√		
Treats all team members fairly and equitably in accordance with the principles of equality and diversity	√		
Managing Tasks and Workload	√		
Prioritizes effectively and ensures that tasks are completed on time	√		
Anticipates potential problems and develops plans to tackle them	√		

Financial Awareness			
Applies product and service knowledge to maximize sales and profits	√		
Ensures that the team achieves high levels of sales and meets targets	√		
Manages budgets to remain within planned expenditure	√		

The Application Form

Your next decision is to decide whether to ask candidates to submit a Curriculum Vitae (CV), an application form, or both. Table 2.1 below sets out the advantages and disadvantages of each.

Table 2.1 Application form or Curriculum Vitae?

	Advantages	Disadvantages
Application form	Standard format for all applicants. Tailored to the specific requirements of the job. Easier for panel members to assess fairly and equally.	May provide less information about the applicant than a detailed CV.
CV	Provides detailed information about the candidate.	Formats will vary between applicants. May contain some irrelevant detail. Harder to identify relevant information and to assess against your criteria.
Both	Double the information!	Double the reading! Duplication of information.

In most instances I recommend using an application form, possibly accompanied by a CV if the nature of the post means that you require a particularly detailed and thorough picture of the applicants.

The application form should be sent to applicants with the job description and the person specification. It should contain the following sections:

Important Information for Applicants

This might include information on how to complete the application, including drawing applicants' attention to the requirements set out in the person specification. You might also highlight any particularly significant policies or priorities, such as your organization's commitment to equality and diversity.

Personal Details

Basic personal information about the applicant such as name and contact details.

Experience

The purpose of this section is firstly to get information about the applicant's career history, but secondly to see how this relates to the requirements of the job. To avoid getting lengthy lists of vaguely relevant details you should be quite clear at the start of this section about the information you are looking for. This may be broken down into three parts:

1. The applicant's *experience.*
2. The applicant's *knowledge*—how they have applied it in their current and previous roles?
3. The applicant's *achievements*—what results have they achieved as a result of applying and implementing their knowledge?

The most important of these elements when it comes to assessing applicants is part 3—their achievements. An applicant may have all the experience and knowledge in the world, but they will not be an asset to your business unless they can apply it to achieve results.

Competencies

This is the section where applicants can provide specific evidence of their ability to demonstrate the competencies set out in the person specification. When designing this section of the application form it is important to be clear about:

1. What the key skills and attributes are
2. How the applicants should demonstrate their ability to meet them

A heading such as "People Management" tells the applicant that this will be an important aspect of the job, but to enable them to provide meaningful evidence of their skills and attributes in this area we need to be more specific about which aspects of people management are particularly important to the job. This can be done by highlighting key bullet points from the person specification, for example:

- Able to manage both good and poor performance.
- Develops effective working relationships with colleagues.
- Communicates effectively with colleagues at all levels.

This provides clarity of what is required, both for applicants completing the forms and for panel members when they are assessing them.

It is also important to provide applicants with information about how you want them to present their evidence. Providing a word limit will encourage them to be succinct and to the point, and again help panel members when reading the forms. Applicants who fail to remain within the stated limits may have their applications rejected—after all, do you want to employ someone who demonstrates that they are unable to follow simple instructions?

You need to make it clear to applicants that you expect them to provide *specific examples* of how they have met the criteria. Every applicant will claim to have "excellent people skills"—what you need to see is specific evidence to substantiate that claim.

Technical Skills

The post you are looking to fill may require specific technical skills, such as the ability to use IT. The application form should ask applicants to provide relevant information about their experience, and also state clearly if skills will be tested.

References

Applicants should be asked to provide the names of two referees. If they have recently been employed then at least one of the referees should be able to comment directly on their performance at work. References should only be taken up for candidates who have reached the required standard at interview. The purpose of taking up references is to confirm that the information provided by candidates on their applications and at interview is accurate.

In the light of this it should be possible to reassure applicants that references will not be requested until after the interview, avoiding the risk of placing them in an awkward position with their current employers.

Closing Statement

Let the candidate know any important information that has not yet been covered, such as when and how you will be contacting them, and dates when they should be available for interview.

Close the application form by thanking the applicant for taking the time and trouble to complete it.

The following is an example of an application form.

Example: Application form

Application Form: Customer Services Manager

Important Information for Applicants

The person specification sets out the criteria that are essential or desirable for this job. Where the method of assessment is stated to be the application form, your application needs to demonstrate clearly and concisely how you meet each of the criteria, even if other methods of assessment are also shown. If you do not address these criteria fully, or if we do not consider that you meet them, you will not be shortlisted. Please give specific examples wherever possible.

Equality and Diversity

We are committed to and champion equality and diversity in all aspects of our work. All employees are expected to understand and promote our equality and diversity policy in the course of their work.

---

1   Personal details

Name	
Contact address	
Contact telephone number(s)	Daytime: Evening: Mobile:
E-mail address	

2   Experience

Give brief details of your experience and your achievements, beginning with your current or most recent post. You should demonstrate how your experience meets the following requirements:

- Successful experience of working and managing people in a busy customer-facing environment.
- Has had to work within budgets.
- Has worked in a sales environment.
- Has recruited people.

Dates	Post held	Brief details of experience and achievements

3.   Competencies

These are the skills and attributes required to perform the duties of this role effectively.

Provide specific examples of no more than 200 words to demonstrate how you meet each of the following criteria.

Developing Customer Relations
- Attracts new customers by promoting products and services.
- Builds and maintains effective relationships with customers.
- Ensures team members provide a consistently high standard of customer service.
- Promptly resolves problems for customers if things go wrong.

Communicating Effectively
- Presents influentially to a wide range of people.
- Listens well and encourages two-way communication.
- Ensures that communication is understood through use of questioning and clarifying skills.

Managing People
- Motivates team members to achieve and maintain high levels of performance.
- Tackles poor performance promptly and effectively.
- Treats all team members fairly and equitably in accordance with the principles of equality and diversity.

Managing Tasks and Workload
- Prioritizes effectively and ensures that tasks are completed on time.
- Anticipates potential problems and develops plans to tackle them.

Financial Awareness
- Applies product and service knowledge to maximize sales and profits.
- Ensures that the team achieves high levels of sales and meets targets.
- Manages budgets to remain within planned expenditure.

4   Qualifications

The successful applicant will need to be educated to degree level or able to demonstrate success in a similar position. You will also require the other qualifications listed below.

Qualifications at degree level or above.*	

5   Other Requirements

Current US driving license*	
Current CRB check*	

*Copies will be required.

6   References

Please provide the name and contact details of two referees, at least one of whom should be able to comment directly on your performance at work.

Please note that referees will only be contacted if you demonstrate the required criteria at interview.

Referee 1	Referee 2
Name: Address: Job Title (if applicable): Daytime phone no.: E-mail:	Name: Address: Job Title (if applicable): Daytime phone no.: E-mail:

Thank you for applying for this post. We will contact you by e-mail by [INSERT DATE] *to let you know whether you are invited for interview.*

Submitting the Application Form

You will need to decide whether applicants should apply online, by e-mail, or by returning a traditional paper application form.

Online or e-mail applications have become the norm over recent years. An online application may be completed via a link to your company's website. Alternatively an application form may be downloaded to the applicant's computer, then returned by e-mail.

Both of these approaches have the advantages of making the process more manageable, and reducing the amount of paper involved. This has both logistical and environmental benefits. Application forms can more easily be submitted by applicants, then made available to the people involved in the process who need to see them.

Bear in mind, however, that not everyone is IT literate, and not everyone has easy access to a computer. If you are recruiting for a sector where IT access and skills are not a core requirement (e.g., some roles in sectors such as construction or cleaning), you may decide to accept paper applications alongside those submitted online or by e-mail.

Panel Member Rating Form

When the application forms are returned you will need a form that enables panel members to identify which applicants meet the standard required to be invited for interview. A well-designed form is more likely to achieve consistency between panel members, and can be used to rate candidates both at the sift and interview stages.

The form should include a rating scale, which is clear and straightforward for panel members to understand and use. An example rating scale is set out below:

Score	Definition
0	Applicant has not provided any relevant evidence of this criteria
1	Applicant has provided insufficient evidence of this criteria to meet the required standard
2	Applicant has provided sufficient evidence of this criteria to meet the required standard
3	Applicant has provided strong evidence of this criteria to exceed the required standard

A key phrase here is "the required standard." The job description and person specification will help to define this, but panel members will all have their own views based upon their own knowledge and experience of the job. The process by which panel members reach agreement on which applicants to invite for interview is covered in Chapter 4—Sifting and Shortlisting.

Unlike the first three forms covered in this chapter, the panel member rating form is a document for internal use only, and will not normally be seen by the candidate. However, you may be required to release the completed forms in the event of any complaint about the way in which the panel has been conducted, if it results in an internal investigation or legal action. In some organizations you will be required to file this documentation with HR at the end of the recruitment process.

I have included an example of a panel member rating form below.

Example: Panel member rating form

Panel Member Rating Form
Name of Applicant:
Date:
Sift/Interview (Please delete as appropriate)

Please rate each criteria in accordance with the following rating scale:

Score	Definition
0	Applicant has not provided any relevant evidence of this criteria
1	Applicant has provided insufficient evidence of this criteria to meet the required standard
2	Applicant has provided sufficient evidence of this criteria to meet the required standard
3	Applicant has provided strong evidence of this criteria to exceed the required standard

Criteria	Score	Comments
Relevant Knowledge and Experience		
Total		

Signed:

Name:

Date:

The Panel Rating Form

The panel rating form is used to record the individual ratings of the panel members, along with the final ratings they have arrived at after discussing the candidate's evidence. The comments should provide a brief reflection of the discussion and reasons for the rating, for example:

Panel member A initially felt that the evidence presented was insufficient, but agreed a rating of 2 after taking into account evidence presented in other sections of the form.

Panel rating forms should be signed by all panel members and retained as the formal record of the agreed ratings and how they were reached.

The panel rating form may be used both when sifting applications to draw up the shortlist for interview and again when rating the candidate's performance at the interview.

I have included an example of a panel rating form below.

Example: Panel Rating Form

Name of Applicant:
Date:
Sift/Interview (Please delete as appropriate)

Please rate each criteria in accordance with the following rating scale:

Score	Definition
0	Applicant has not provided any relevant evidence of this criteria
1	Applicant has provided insufficient evidence of this criteria to meet the required standard
2	Applicant has provided sufficient evidence of this criteria to meet the required standard
3	Applicant has provided strong evidence of this criteria to exceed the required standard

Criteria	Chair	Member A	Member B	Panel's Agreed Rating
Total				

Comments and Reasons for the agreed rating:

Signed:
Chair:
Member A:
Member B:
Date:

Storage of Forms and Confidentiality of Information

All documents completed as part of a recruitment and selection process must be stored confidentially, and in accordance with regulations regarding protection of personal data.

Electronic documents must be stored on a secure system and be password protected. Any paper documents must be securely locked away.

Documents should be retained centrally and securely to provide a full record of the recruitment process. They may be required in future, for example, if an applicant wishes to make an appeal if they feel the process has not be conducted fairly.

Organizations sometimes retain applications completed by unsuccessful applicants in case a similar vacancy arises in the future. You need to let applicants know if this is the case and obtain their permission for their applications to be retained for a specified period of time, for example, six months. Your organization should have a process for checking and ensuring that documents are removed and destroyed after the specified period of time.

Summary of Chapter 2—Laying the Foundations

In this chapter I have discussed how to lay the foundations for successful recruitment by:

- Writing the job description.
- Writing the person specification.
- Devising the application form.
- Drawing up the panel member rating form.
- Drawing up the overall panel rating form.
- Ensuring that documentation is stored securely and that personal data are protected.

CHAPTER 3

Advertising the Vacancy

This chapter covers how to find and attract candidates, where to advertise, how to advertise, what to include in the advertisement, and drafting the advertisement.

Finding and Attracting Candidates

Having a current job description and person specification is important, but it won't get you anywhere unless it reaches the right people. The next stage in the process is thinking about where those potential candidates are, and how to let them know that you are recruiting.

Before advertising a vacancy externally think about potential internal candidates, existing employees who meet the requirements of the person specification you have prepared for the role. Advertising internally demonstrates that promotion and development are encouraged, which is motivational for your existing workforce.

If you have sufficient potential candidates within your organization, you may decide only to advertise the vacancy internally. However, this runs the risk of creating a stagnant, inward-looking organizational culture, with insufficient understanding of the needs of your customers and new initiatives being taken by your competitors. External recruitment helps to address this, by bringing different approaches and perspectives into your organization.

A balanced approach may be not only to encourage internal candidates to apply for the vacancy, but also to open it up to a wider pool of candidates by advertising externally.

Your organization should also have a record of previous applicants. These may be people who have applied for vacancies in the past, or people who have contacted your organization because they wish to work for you. This latter group may be a great source of potential employees; they have shown both a desire to work for your organization and initiative in contacting you.

Another source of potential candidates may be local schools and colleges, particularly if they run courses that are relevant to your business. Training and education providers may also deliver relevant courses and qualifications, and have students who are potential employees. This may be particularly helpful if the job role requires a relevant qualification.

You may be able to advertise through relevant professional bodies, on their websites or in their journals. Trade and business magazines will also carry advertisements, which again will enable you to target potential applicants. These journals and magazines also require content, and providing articles for them is a great way of raising awareness about your business and what it does, and may lead to people contacting you about potential vacancies.

Recruitment agencies will be able to provide you with plenty of potential employees, but you will need to ensure that they are fully aware of the specific requirements of the role for which you are recruiting. A good recruitment agency will help you to identify and shortlist the right candidates. You will need to balance the costs involved against the savings in time, and also consider whether you wish to control which candidates reach the interview stage, or hand this part of the process over to the agency.

Finally, the Internet is a great source of potential candidates, but again you need to use it strategically to ensure that you reach the right people. Your organization should advertise vacancies on its website, and may use social media to reach potential candidates and direct them to the advertisement. Online jobsites have become increasingly popular. Ensure that you get good value for money by using those which are most relevant to your business.

Where to Advertise?

You will need to target your advertising so that it reaches the potential candidates you wish to attract for your business. Options include:

- Listing vacancies on your corporate website.
- Social media sites such as LinkedIn, Facebook, Twitter, and YouTube.

- Internet recruitment sites/job boards.
- Local or national newspapers.
- Specialist publications from professional bodies or trade associations.

You will probably need to utilize a combination of these channels in order to reach the maximum number of potential candidates.

How to Advertise?

How you advertise depends on the type of candidate you are trying to attract. Using YouTube is more likely to reach younger, more digitally aware candidates; using trade journals is more likely to reach candidates with greater experience and professional qualifications.

You may be very clear about the type of candidate you wish to attract. In this case you can be more targeted in the way you advertise. However, if you wish to attract a diverse range of candidates, you will need to use a wider range of advertising methods.

In a crowded marketplace you may need to use creative methods to get your company and your vacancy noticed, and putting videos on social media such as Facebook or YouTube will help you to achieve this. However, don't forget that at some point potential candidates will need detailed information about the job, so whatever form of advertising you use it will need to clearly direct them to where they can find the job description, person specification, and application form.

You will also need to consider how much you wish to spend on advertising the vacancy. You should set a budget for advertising, and make sure you keep to this. When setting this, you need to consider how much it is reasonable to spend, considering the level of the job. In some circumstances, such as a major recruitment campaign or the recruitment of a senior member of staff, it may be worth investing significant money in your advertising campaign. In other circumstances it may be possible to spend less, and still reach the right candidates for the job. A key question to ask is:

What kind of advertising will reach the candidates we want—at the least possible cost?

What to Include in the Advertisement?

Draw up a checklist of what prospective candidates will need to know. This may include:

- The name and nature of your organization.
- Its purpose and core values.
- Job title.
- The nature of the job and its main responsibilities.
- How the job relates to others in the organization.
- Where the job is located.
- Education and qualifications required.
- Specific abilities/competencies required.
- Any relevant physical or health requirements.
- Any age restrictions.
- Pay and other benefits.
- Working conditions.
- Who to contact for further information.
- How to apply.
- Closing date for applications.

This would be a lot of information to include in an advertisement! The advertisement should contain "headline" information, designed to grab the reader's attention by letting them know that you are offering an exciting job opportunity, and that your organization is a great place to work. The rest of the detail should be put into a separate information sheet, which you can make available online or send to prospective applicants.

Drafting the Advertisement

Decide whether you and other colleagues have the skills and knowledge required to draw up the advertisement. If you have an in-house HR department, specialized HR personnel will most likely take on this task, but make sure that you are involved in the process. In the case of a senior post, or if you are recruiting for a large number of posts, you may wish to hire a recruitment agency to draft and place the advertisement. Ensure that it provides the details set out above.

Make sure that the advertisement presents a positive picture of your organization. Including information about its purpose and core values is more likely to attract suitable candidates. You will also need to ensure that the advertisement complies with relevant legislation.

Your advertisement should include details of how potential candidates can obtain further information. For a small recruitment campaign this may be a named contact and their telephone number, so that people can have an informal conversation about the post before deciding whether to apply. For a larger campaign you may offer the opportunity for people to attend informal information sessions, where they would be given a presentation about the company and the opportunity to talk to existing employees. The advertisement should also direct people to further information available on your organization's website.

Respondents to the advertisement should be sent the job description, person specification, application form, and relevant information about your organization, its terms and conditions of employment, and the application process.

Drafting Your Advertisement—Some Top Tips

- Make your advertisement visually interesting. An advertisement that catches the eye is more likely to be noticed, and makes your company seem more appealing. Consider employing a graphic designer to help you with this.
- Make sure the job title accurately reflects the role. If you want to recruit a marketing expert then advertise for a marketing expert, don't invent a title like "marketing guru." Other titles may be meaningful to those already in the company but meaningless to external candidates—"modality manager" and "surveyorship enumerator" are two I have seen recently (for the record, the modality manager is a senior nurse, while the surveyorship enumerator counted cars going through traffic lights).
- Avoid general or meaningless requirements, such as "Good with people." Most applicants will think that they are good with people, so it is important to be more specific about the

qualities required in the particular role. A counselor would need to be able to "listen and demonstrate empathy," whereas a leader might need to be able to "motivate and enthuse team members."

- Be careful about the words you choose to describe the qualities required to do the job. "Gravitas," for example, is a word which is often associated with older men, so using this word in a job advertisement might deter younger people or women from applying. Remember that broadening the appeal of a job will enable you to select from a wider cross-section of applicants.

- Advertising for a "recent graduate" discriminates against older candidates, while specifying "10 years' experience required" will discriminate against younger ones. Ask yourself whether it is really necessary to apply these conditions and, if possible, avoid them.

- Make it clear if your company offers flexible working patterns. There may be a full-time post to be filled, but there may be a variety of ways in which that can be achieved. These may include two people job-sharing, or one person working condensed hours, spread over a four-day week or a nine-day fortnight. Will the successful applicant always have to be in the office, or is there scope for working from home? There is scope for far more flexibility than everyone working the traditional nine to five, five days a week.

Summary of Chapter 3—Advertising the Vacancy

In this chapter I have covered the importance of advertising your vacancy in a way which will reach, and appeal to, the right people. This includes considering:

- How to find and attract the right candidates.
- Where to advertise your vacancy.
- How to advertise your vacancy, and which medium will enable you to reach potential applicants.

- What to include in your advertisement, and what information to provide separately.
- How to draft the advertisement, including some tips on what to include and what to avoid.

CHAPTER 4

Sifting and Shortlisting

This chapter covers setting the initial sift criteria, conducting the initial sift—automatic and manual approaches, conducting the second sift, and shortlisting for interview.

The Sift is your opportunity to scrutinize the written evidence submitted by the candidate, and to decide whether it justifies progressing them to the interview stage. In order to do this you will need to systematically evaluate the evidence they have provided for each area of the person specification, and assess each area in accordance with the agreed rating scale (see Chapter 2—Laying the Foundations).

This chapter firstly sets out the process for doing this, and then provides guidance on successful sifting, including guarding against bias and overcoming problems which may arise at the sifting stage. The chapter concludes by looking at how to notify the results to both successful and unsuccessful applicants.

The Sifting Process

The sifting process can be divided into three stages:

1. *The initial sift*, which identifies and removes candidates who do not meet the basic specified criteria for the post, or who have failed to complete the application form correctly. This can be done manually, but automated sifting tools may be quicker and more efficient.
2. *The individual stage*, where panel members scrutinize the applications that have passed the initial sift and come to their own initial assessments.
3. *The collective stage*, where they will meet as a panel and decide which candidates should be invited for interview.

The Initial Sift

Options for carrying out the initial sift include:

- Getting your administrative team to check whether minimum criteria have been met. For example: Does the applicant have the required qualifications? Have they completed the application forms correctly and completely? Have they remained within specified word limits?
- Using artificial intelligence (AI), in the form of an automated sifting tool, to identify whether candidates have met basic criteria. The tool may also check whether their applications contain predefined "key words," which would indicate their suitability for interview. Some tools included "situational judgment" tests, where applicants are presented with a situation then asked to select which of a number of multiple choice responses would be most appropriate.
- Sifting against one "lead competency," which has been identified as an essential requirement for the job. If candidates do not demonstrate this competency to the required standard then they can be sifted out of the process.
- Splitting the applications between panel members instead of each panel member looking at all of them. The sift discussion can then focus on the highest scoring candidates identified by each member.

The use of automated sifting tools has become increasingly popular. It is easy to purchase software that will automate this time-consuming and labor-intensive stage of the process, enabling sifting to be carried out efficiently and easily. However, there is a question mark against the effectiveness of these processes. Stories abound of in-house candidates, who have often already demonstrated their ability to do the job, being sifted out of the selection process because they have failed to select the right answers to multiple choice situational questions, or to use the required "key words" in their responses. This reduces the test to a game of "guess the right answer," instead of being a true reflection of the applicant's judgment.

The other issue with using AI in recruitment and selection is the question of who is coding the algorithms, and what criteria are they being coded to look for? In October 2018, it was widely publicized that Amazon abandoned a recruitment platform that was found to favor male candidates, and penalized applications that contained the words "woman" or "women." The platform's algorithms had developed measures of success from the curricula vitae (CVs) of people who had been successful in the Tech sector, which historically has been a male-dominated industry. And the algorithms were coded by people already working in the sector, predominantly young men. So there is a risk that using automated sifting tools will perpetuate the status quo, and reflect the (often unconscious) biases of their creators.

The Individual Stage

At the start of the individual stage it is important for panel members to discuss how to score the application forms. This might involve discussing the type of evidence required to justify the ratings required at each level for each of the criteria. Having this discussion at the start of the process encourages consistency of approach between panel members, reduces the range of individual scores, and will usually save time at the collective stage. It is particularly helpful to do this if the panel includes members who are sifting applications for the first time.

You will need:

- Your own set of application forms (either electronic or paper copies).
- Panel member rating forms.

Set aside sufficient time to read through and mark all of the application forms. If there are not too many try and do this at a single sitting. This will help you to focus on the criteria and assess the evidence presented by each candidate fairly and equally.

As you read through the forms you will find it helpful to:

- *Highlight* sections or statements which provide key evidence of the candidate's ability to meet or not meet the criteria.

- *Annotate* the forms with notes—for example, of questions arising from the evidence provided that you may wish to follow up at interview.
- *Note* on the panel member rating form your initial score for each of the criteria.

Remember that at this stage the scores you are recording are only your *initial ratings*, in order to provide a basis for discussion with your colleagues when you meet as a panel. You may subsequently change these initial ratings following discussion, for example, if one of your colleagues has identified a piece of relevant evidence that you may have missed.

The Collective Stage

Once you have individually scored the applications you should meet as a panel to decide which candidates will go through to the next stage of the process. You will need to decide at the outset the minimum requirements for this. Applying the rating scale we are using here, for example, you may decide that the minimum requirement for an applicant to be considered for interview is a score for each criteria of:

2—Applicant has provided sufficient evidence of the criteria to meet the required standard

You will also need to consider how many applicants you wish to interview. If you only have one vacancy to fill, it is unlikely that you will want to spend more than one day interviewing. If this is the case you may decide only to interview the four or five highest scoring candidates—as long as they score a rating of at least 2 for each of the criteria. As you will see in Chapter 5—Preparing for the Interview—I recommend that you should not try and conduct more than five interviews in a day.

We have now identified the requirements for being invited to interview as:

- Must score a rating of at least 2 for each of the criteria.
- Must be one of the top five highest rated candidates.

When you meet as a panel you will need to consider each applicant in turn. The chairperson should ask the panel members for their ratings and record these on the panel member rating form. The panel should then discuss the ratings given for each candidate.

Particular attention should be given to areas where panel members disagree.

In these instances the chairperson should lead a structured discussion on the evidence considered by each panel member which led to their decision. The aim of the discussion should be to reach an agreed rating as a panel. When doing this remember that the person in the minority may be the one with the right rating—they may have identified positive or negative evidence that their two colleagues have missed.

At the end of the sift meeting the following papers should be attached together for each candidate:

- Overall panel rating form.
- Panel member rating forms completed by the individual members.
- Application form.

The applications should be separated into two clear piles:

- Candidates to be invited to interview.
- Candidates not to be invited to interview.

Ensuring Effective Sifting

Consider the evidence from the whole of the form when scoring the applicants. There will be overlaps between the criteria; for example, a candidate's evidence for their ability to communicate effectively may also provide evidence of their ability to provide excellent customer service. It is therefore important to read the whole form before scoring candidates and to take all the available evidence into account.

Develop a system for sifting—for example, using different colors to highlight positive and negative evidence, or areas that you might wish to follow up with questions at interview. Using a system consistently will help you when it comes to the sift discussion and preparing for inter-view. Ideally, for ease of reference, all panel members should use the same system.

Look critically at the evidence provided. Application forms and CVs provide a useful initial guide to the candidates' capabilities, but cannot provide the depth of evidence which arises in an interview.

Beware of candidates simply restating the criteria set out in the person specification. For example, for "Financial Awareness" a candidate may write

> I always ensure that I remain within planned expenditure by care-fully managing my budgets. I maximize sales and profits by keep-ing my product and service knowledge up to date and sharing this with my team. By doing this I ensure that the team consistently achieves its sales targets.

This may initially look impressive, but does not provide specific evi-dence of anything the candidate has actually done. They have identified from the person specification what they think you want to read, and then simply rehashed it. You should also beware of candidates who overuse the latest management buzz words. They may claim to be "an outstanding leader with a strategic perspective and commitment to achieving excellent results through empowering the team"—but have they actually provided any evidence that backs this up?

Guarding Against Bias

We have already seen how bias can creep into automated selection pro-cesses but—guess what? It affects humans too. In Chapter 6, we will discuss the potential impact of this, and how to guard against it, at the interview stage. However, it may also affect decisions made when sifting and shortlisting.

Here are some of the types of bias to guard against.

- *The halo effect*

This refers to the tendency to allow things we like about an applicant to affect our judgment about other factors. This is particularly evident if we perceive someone as having similar attributes to ourselves; at a sub-conscious level the brain is thinking "This looks like just the right person for the job!"—before we even meet them and start testing their evidence.

- *The horns effect*

This is the opposite of the halo effect, when we allow something we dislike about an applicant to affect our judgment. This may be something specific to the candidate—at the interview stage there may be things we don't like about their appearance, their accent, or the way in which they present themselves, which prompts a subconscious negative reaction. At the sifting and shortlisting stage it may be something as simple as their name, prompting subconscious stereotypical assumptions about the ability of "that type of person" to do a good job.

- *Confirmation bias*

The halo and horns effects are forms of confirmation bias, where we look for evidence to confirm a pre-existing belief or hypothesis. Human beings love to prove themselves right, so it's very tempting to look for evidence that enables you to say "I knew that was the right candidate as soon as I saw their application form!" The problem with confirmation bias is that it impairs our judgment, and inhibits our ability to treat all candidates fairly and equally.

- *Transference*

Transference arises when you transfer the characteristics of one person on to another. For example, there may be things in a candidate's application which remind you of a previous employee who did a really great job for you in a similar role. This leads our subconscious brain to leap to the conclusion "This person sounds just like Julie! She's going to be great!" Of course, the opposite can apply, and we may leap to negative assumptions—"I had a Bob from Wisconsin working for me before. He was useless!" As with the other forms of bias, there is then the risk of looking for evidence to prove these initial judgments were correct.

- *Successive contrasting bias*

This arises when someone who appears to be an outstanding candidate causes recruiters to negatively judge others who are assessed after them. At the sift you may judge subsequent candidates more harshly if they do not appear to meet this standard, while at the interview evidence suggests that as many as the next three candidates are assessed more harshly compared with the outstanding candidate. The problem at the sifting stage is exacerbated as you are only making judgments on the basis of written evidence. A candidate may have provided an impressive application, but the interview and other assessment processes may reveal that there is little substance behind it.

Over recent years there has been increasing awareness of the potential impact of bias in processes such as recruitment and selection, and many organizations have taken steps to guard against it. These include:

- *Unconscious bias training*

Many organizations now provide training that aims to enable people to become aware of their unconscious or subconscious biases, and guard against acting on these when doing their jobs. It is important that people involved in the recruitment process attend this training, and are open to recognizing and addressing forms of bias in themselves. Bias can affect all stages of the process, from the criteria laid down in the job advertisement, through to decisions made at the sifting, shortlisting, and interview stages.

- *Notice the first thought, act on the second*

An important principle I learned from attending unconscious bias training is to "notice the first thought, act on the second." For example, a candidate with an unusually spelt name, "Aimee" instead of "Amy," or "Baylee" instead of "Bailey," may lead a recruiter to make assumptions about that person's social class, their levels of education, or literacy. Those assumptions might be their first thought, but hopefully the second thought will be along the lines of "Hold on! It's the parents who came up with the name, not the applicant! And maybe they had good reasons for spelling it that way, which we don't know about." So this process of noticing the first thought, then acting on the second, is a good way of safeguarding ourselves from acting upon bias or unfounded prejudice.

- *Challenging groupthink*

There is a danger of groupthink in recruitment, where biased decisions are made because all the panel members are thinking in the same way. Ensuring that you have diverse panels is a way of guarding against this. Panels should always include someone from outside the line management chain for the post, and often benefit from including a representative from the HR Department. Other points to consider include gender balance, black and ethnic minority representation, and demonstrating that your organization has a positive and enabling approach to including people with disabilities.

- *Blind recruitment*

Some organizations have taken the view that all this is best addressed through a process of "blind recruitment," where information such as the candidate's name, gender, age, and educational background is omitted until they reach the interview stage. This means that decisions about who to shortlist should solely be based on the evidence they have provided about their ability to do the job.

Blind recruitment is often perceived as a recent innovation but it was first used by the Boston Symphony Orchestra, right back in 1952. The musicians in the orchestra were predominantly male; so, in a bid to create a level playing field for female musicians, candidates were asked to audition behind a screen, to ensure that they were being judged purely on their ability, not on their gender. Subsequent studies suggested that this increased the likelihood of women being hired by up to 46 percent.

However, there are mixed views on the effectiveness of blind recruitment in addressing discrimination. Jozsef Blasko, HR director at Coca-Cola Eastern Europe, says:

> Blind recruitment is a very stupid way of trying to eliminate bias. The whole point of recruitment is to take everything into account, so using blind recruitment as an equal opportunities approach defeats the very purpose of hiring.

Blasko gives the example of a white, male candidate who has built up an impressive CV. If his success is partly due to the unconscious bias of previous recruiters and mangers, then blind recruitment will work in his favor, and against the interests of candidates who have not had these advantages. So there is a risk that blind recruitment will perpetuate discrimination instead of eliminating it.

While we should aim to ensure that recruitment processes are as fair and open as possible, eliminating bias and discrimination completely is likely to remain an unattainable Holy Grail. Any process involving human beings, or technology programmed by human beings, will probably contain some degree of bias. But everyone involved in recruitment has a responsibility to minimize this, by being willing to take a critical look at themselves, their colleagues, and the processes they are being asked to follow and, where necessary, being willing to follow through and take action to make the process as fair and open as it can possibly be.

Sifting Problems

The following problems may need to be addressed at the Sift stage:

- *Too many applications*

Your options for dealing with this problem may depend on when it is identified. If you realize at an early stage that you are receiving more applications than expected, it may be possible to withdraw your advertising and bring forward the closing date for applications. If it is not possible to do this, or the problem is not spotted until later, using an automatic sifting tool, or bringing in administrative support, will help you sift a large number of applications quickly.

- *Too many good quality applications*

You may have a number of applicants with similar scores, making it difficult to decide who to invite for interview. If this is the case you may wish to consider including an additional stage in the process, between the Sift and the interview. This may take the form of short telephone interviews, targeted at the key criteria, in order to identify the leading candidates from your shortlist. Alternatively you may introduce additional tests before the interview stage.

- *A shortfall of good quality applications*

While it may be tempting to interview the "least bad" applicants, if they do not meet the minimum criteria set for interview they are unlikely to be the quality of candidates you are looking for. You may wish to consider factors such as the wording, presentation, and placement of your advertising and then re-advertise the post. It may be frustrating to have to delay the process, but it is better to address the problem at this stage than to continue in the vain hope that one of your unpromising candidates will suddenly display hitherto unseen qualities at interview. As highlighted in the Introduction, the costs of appointing the wrong candidate, in terms of money, time, and efficiency, are considerable.

Notifying Sift Results to Applicants

Once you have reached your decisions about who to invite to interview, you need to notify the applicants. When notifying unsuccessful applicants it is important to remember that they are likely to be disappointed. They have demonstrated a desire to work in your organization and probably put a good deal of time and effort into completing the application form. It is therefore important to be sensitive in the wording of the letter, in order to leave them with a positive impression of your organization and a feeling of having been treated respectfully and fairly.

You may also wish to offer them the opportunity to receive feedback on why their application has been unsuccessful. If you decide to do this you need to include information on how this feedback will be provided. You may wish to encourage the candidate to take the initiative, in which case they will need to know who to contact and when to contact them.

Feedback will normally be provided by phone. If you are the panel member responsible for doing this ensure that you have the sift papers to hand. When providing feedback you will need to strike the right balance between being positive and encouraging, for example, by recognizing areas where the applicant scored well, while being very clear about where there were gaps between the evidence they presented and the required standard.

If you have a large number of unsuccessful applicants it may save time if you provide brief feedback in the letter.

Applicants who have been successful at the sift stage should be invited to attend the next stage of the process, and be asked to confirm their attendance. It is good practice for advertisements to include interview dates so that applicants can keep their diaries free. If it was not possible to do this then the letter should give applicants at least two weeks' notice of the interview date.

The letter to a candidate being invited to interview will need to include:

- Time and place of interview.
- Length of interview.
- Names and job titles of panel members.
- Instructions on what to do on arrival.
- Details of any documents they are required to bring (e.g., certificates).
- Details of any additional aspects of the selection process (e.g., IT tests, presentations, psychometric tests, etc.).

Summary of Chapter 4—Sifting and Shortlisting

This chapter has identified what is required at three stages of sifting: the initial sift, the individual stage, and the collective stage. Use of an automated sifting tool is an option which might be considered at the initial stage, if there are a large number of applications to be sifted.

It is important that anyone involved in sifting takes steps to guard against their decisions being influenced by unconscious or subconscious biases. We have identified five forms of bias, and how to minimize the risks of allowing them to affect your assessment decisions.

We have identified some of the problems that may arise at the Sift stage and how to overcome them. Finally, the chapter sets out how to notify Sift results to both successful and unsuccessful candidates.

CHAPTER 5

Preparing for the Interview

This chapter covers creating the right environment for the interview, the interview timetable, defining and agreeing panel members' roles, the interview plan, preparing your questions, and timekeeping.

I will cover what needs to be done to:

- Create the right environment for the interviews.
- Draw up the interview timetable.
- Define and agree panel members' roles and responsibilities.
- Draw up the interview plan.
- Prepare the interview questions.
- Make effective use of video interviewing.

Creating the Right Environment

Creating the right environment begins with ensuring that interview candidates are able to easily find their way to your office and, when they do, that they are able to get into the building and find their way to the right part of it! Transport and car parking arrangements should also be made clear. This information should be included in the letter inviting candidates to interview.

On the day of the interview ensure that Security or Reception staff have written details of who is attending and when. Ensure that they are clear about where to direct candidates when they arrive. Consider appointing a member of your team as a "meeter and greeter," who can welcome the candidates and take them to the waiting area. This should be a quiet, comfortable area with hot drinks and water available and easy access to toilet facilities. Advance consideration of these points will create an environment where your candidates can prepare to give their best in the interview.

The interview room should be quiet and free from distractions. Make sure any phones in the room are disconnected or switched off before you start interviewing. This includes your cell phones! A candidate has the right to expect you to give them your full attention for the duration of the interview, so only check your phones during breaks. It is good practice for the chairperson to remind panel members to switch off their phones before the interviews begin. Candidates should also be reminded to switch off their phones at the start of the interview.

Make sure the environment is conducive to an effective interview. Any displays on the walls should be appropriate to your organization. Lighting should be bright, but not harsh. If the interview room has windows then check that the sun is not shining directly into anyone's eyes. Take a moment to sit in the candidate's chair. Are there any distractions from that position, which are not visible from where the panel members are sitting?

It is important to set up the interview room in a way which is appropriate to your organization and the nature of the post to be filled. For example, if your company works in the creative sector, it may be appropriate to create a very informal environment for the interview, with soft seating and low, unobtrusive coffee tables. At the other end of the spectrum there is the traditional formal environment, with the panel members sitting facing the interviewee from behind a desk. The two options are illustrated below.

Generally speaking candidates are more likely to talk openly if they feel relaxed, and this is more likely to be the case in an informal environment. However, this is not the only factor to consider. If you are interviewing for a post in a very formal profession, such as the law, you may wish to create a formal environment in order to see how candidates come across in the type of setting that they will be working in. If you are interviewing candidates for high pressure posts, such as members of a sales team, you may consider that a very relaxed and comfortable environment may not be a good match for the role.

You also need to consider what refreshments to offer candidates. If your aim is to create an informal environment in which candidates will feel welcomed and comfortable you may offer hot drinks and biscuits. If you have already provided these in the waiting area—or if you don't want your candidates to feel too comfortable—you may only provide water. The minimum that should be available is a glass of water for everyone—both candidates and panel members may suffer from a dry throat or mouth during the interview.

Formal Interview Environment

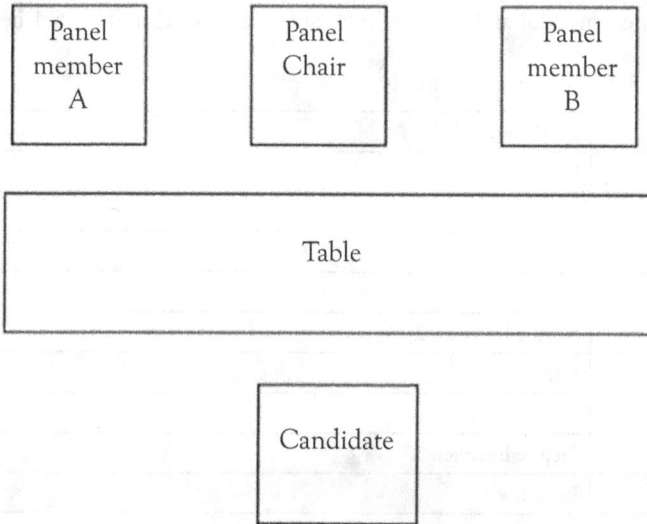

Panel member A	Panel Chair	Panel member B

Table

Candidate

Informal Interview Environment

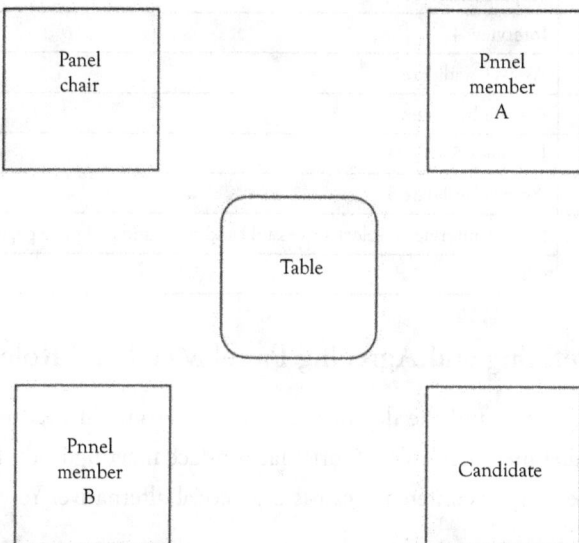

Panel chair	Pnnel member A

Table

Pnnel member B	Candidate

The Interview Timetable

In order to allow sufficient time for preparation and assessment, you should not try to schedule more than four or five interviews in a day. This may be reduced if you are using interviews alongside other selection methods such as presentations or practical exercises, particularly if the panel members are involved in observing these.

An example of an interview timetable is provided in table 5.1 below.

Table 5.1 Interview timetable

9.00	Panel convenes
9.15	Prepare Interview 1
9.30	Interview 1
10.15	Assess Candidate 1
10.30	Break
10.45	Prepare Interview 2
11.00	Interview 2
11.45	Assess Candidate 2
12.00	Prepare Interview 3
12.15	Interview 3
1.00	Assess Candidate 3
1.15	Lunch
2.00	Prepare Interview 4
2.15	Interview 4
3.00	Assess Candidate 4
3.15	Prepare Interview 5
3.30	Interview 5
4.15	Assess Candidate 5
4.30	Review interviews, select successful candidate, and complete paperwork
5.00	Close

Defining and Agreeing Panel Members' Roles

Between the Sift and the day of the interviews you will need to decide on the panel members' roles. A brief face-to-face meeting is ideal, but an online meeting or conference call is a practical alternative. You need to decide:

- Who will test each criteria.
- The order in which each person will lead the questioning.
- Who will take notes at each stage.

This should then be recorded on the interview plan (see below). It is simplest if the same plan is followed for each interview. It may be self-evident as to which panel member should lead the questioning on some of the criteria; for example, if some of the criteria are technical it would make sense for the technical specialist on the panel to lead on these (hopefully he or she will also understand the answers!). However, there may be circumstances where you vary the interview plan. If you are involved in a major selection panel, with interviews taking place over several days, you may swap responsibilities around in order to avoid becoming stale.

The Interview Plan

When drawing up your interview plan pay attention to the sequencing of the interview. In the example below the interview is sequenced to start with areas that the candidate is likely to find easier to talk about, in order to put them at ease and encourage them to talk openly. Most candidates feel comfortable talking about their knowledge and experience, and most candidates will also be able to call to mind examples of Customer Relations—anyone with experience of a customer-facing role will have stories to tell of customers they have found challenging or difficult. The second half of the interview then moves on to cover the more challenging areas, such as Task Management and Financial Awareness.

One approach that has become increasingly popular is to start the interview by asking the candidate to talk about their strengths. Most candidates will have prepared for this, and will be glad of the opportunity to talk about examples of things they have done well. Some organizations do not assess the candidate's answer to this initial strengths-based question, preferring instead to use it as an opportunity to observe their demeanor when they are likely to feel reasonably comfortable providing the answer. This then sets a baseline for the rest of the interview, enabling you to identify when the candidate appears confident and engaged when giving their answers, and the areas where they appear less engaged and confident. It is argued that this is fairer to candidates because you are considering their own demeanor at each stage of the interview, reducing the risk of successive contrasting bias, or of comparing the candidate's demeanor to that of an imaginary "ideal" candidate.

While I think it is helpful to start with a strengths-based question, my own view is that the panel should be assessing the answers right from the start of the interview. Only a finite amount of time is available for the interview, and this should be fully utilized in gathering evidence which will enable you to make a decision as to the best candidate for the role.

Note-taking responsibilities fall to panel members A and B. The chairperson's prime responsibility is to get an overall picture of the candidate and the evidence they provide. This enables the chairperson to identify and note any areas that need following up or investigating further at the end of the interview.

An example interview plan is provided below in Table 5.2.

Table 5.2 Interview plan

Lead responsibility	Time allowed	Criteria to cover	Note taker
Chairperson	10 minutes	Welcome and Introductions Opening strength-based question Criteria 1—Relevant knowledge and experience	Member A
Member A	10–15 minutes	Criteria 2—Customer Relations Criteria 3—Communicating Effectively	Member B
Member B	10–15 minutes	Criteria 4—People Management Skills Criteria 5—Task Management	Member A
Chairperson	10 minutes	Criteria 6—Financial Awareness Any outstanding questions Close the interview	Member B

Preparing Your Questions

Once the interview plan has been devised, each panel member will know which of the criteria they have lead responsibility for testing. They should then review the evidence presented on the candidate's application form, and note the key questions they wish to ask to ensure that the criteria will be fully tested.

This is the point in the process where you can develop questions that are specifically relevant to the evidence provided by the particular candidate. You will draft opening questions starting with phrases such as:

> You mention on your application form ...
> On your application form you gave an example of Customer Relations when ...
> On your application form you talked about a time when you had personal responsibility for a major project ...

Use an interview preparation sheet to *write down* your opening question exactly as you intend to ask it. Remember that you may have to quickly shift gears between the roles of note taker and lead interviewer. You may also feel nervous—it's generally recognized that candidates get nervous, but interviewers do too! Sometimes the effect of these nerves can be that the opening question doesn't come out as clearly as you intended it to, which means that the candidate may set off in the wrong direction because you failed to provide a clear enough steer. Having your opening question written down minimizes the risk of this happening.

Do not write down a long list of questions. The effect of this will be that you spend your time robotically working your way down your list, instead of listening to the candidate's answers. Have a few key questions jotted down as an aide memoire, but once your opening question has sent the candidate moving down the right track, your follow-up questions should simply be prompts to get them to tell you the whole story.

More detailed guidance on formulating and phrasing your questions can be found in Chapters 6 and 7.

A blank interview preparation sheet is shown below.

Interview Preparation Sheet

Complete a separate interview preparation sheet for each of the criteria you are testing.

Criteria:- *People Management*	
• Motivates team members to achieve and maintain high levels of performance. • Tackles poor performance promptly and effectively. • Treats all team members fairly and equitably in accordance with the principles of equality and diversity.	
Opening Question	**Notes**
Possible Follow-up Questions	

A blank interview preparation sheet for your own use can be found at Appendix 8.

Timekeeping

The chairperson has overall responsibility for ensuring that the interview runs to time. This means that they must have clear sight of the time, perhaps a clock on the wall behind the candidate, or a watch discreetly placed on the table. Both of these are preferable to a cell phone—even if it's switched to silent you may be distracted by notifications and messages.

When the time allotted for each member's questions is coming to an end there should be an agreed signal to indicate to the panel member that they should draw their questions to a close. One way of doing this is to have a marker pen on the table, which the chairperson picks up and places in front of the panel member to alert them that their time is nearly up. Candidates are usually far too engrossed in presenting their evidence to notice this!

Summary of Chapter 5—Preparing for the Interview

In this chapter I have covered the importance of thorough preparation before the interviews take place. This includes preparing:

The environment—this includes reception, the waiting area, and setting up the interview room so that it is free from distractions and appropriate to the type of interview you wish to conduct.

The interview timetable—ensuring that everyone knows what is happening and when, and building in sufficient time to prepare for each interview and assess candidates as you go along.

An interview plan, so that panel members are clear about their specific roles and responsibilities.

Time keeping arrangements and signals.

Opening questions, which should specifically relate to the candidate's application and be written down.

CHAPTER 6

Conducting the Interview: The Process

This chapter identifies what panel members need to do in order to conduct a successful interview, and some of the pitfalls to avoid. I will cover:

- How to start the interview on the right note
- How to build rapport with the interviewee
- How to keep the interview on track and fully test the relevant criteria
- Potential pitfalls and how to avoid them
- Closing the interview

Starting the Interview

The opening three minutes of the interview are a crucial time. First impressions may be misleading (more on this when we come on to pitfalls), but are nevertheless important. And while you may be aware of the need to guard against giving undue weight to first impressions, your candidate will be taking in information that will help form their view of you and your company. They will be keen to make a positive impression on you, but if you get things wrong they may begin to doubt whether your organization is one they wish to work for. So, starting an interview badly may not just leave you feeling foolish—it could lead to you losing your best candidate.

The previous chapter, "Preparing for the Interview," covers the importance of briefing your Security and Reception staff and making a comfortable waiting area available. The next point that needs to be clear is how candidates will get from the waiting area to the interview room. You have two main options:

1. Arrange for a member of staff to be available to show them in. The advantage of this approach is that the panel can be ready and in position for the interview to start, creating a professional first impression for the candidate.
2. Have a member of the interview panel collect them from the waiting area and bring them through. The advantage of this approach is that the panel member is able to immediately "break the ice" and begin the process of rapport building before the interview begins.

Once the candidate is in the interview room, the chairperson should first check that it is the right person! Timetabling mix-ups are not unknown, and in a busy building where lots of people are coming and going it is quite possible for people to end up in the wrong places. It's like those occasional mix-ups on TV news programs, where bemused drivers suddenly find themselves in front of the cameras being grilled about the major news stories of the day.

Once you've established that you have the right candidate, check how they wish to be addressed. Do this in a way which invites them to agree with the approach you've chosen to adopt; if you're planning to conduct a fairly informal interview, say something like "So you're Robert Simpson—o.k. if we call you Robert?" If the candidate's reply is, "Well—most people call me Bob"—then go with their preference and call them Bob.

If you're really not sure how to address a candidate, or how to pronounce their name, then ask them! It's better to check at the start than to undermine all your other attempts at rapport building by mispronouncing their name throughout the interview.

The chairperson should also introduce the panel members. If you are using the candidate's first name then it is obviously appropriate to include your first names. Introductions should be along the lines of:

On my *right is Sunita Malik, our HR manager ...*

Pause to give each panel member the chance to smile and say hello—this is an important part of building rapport.

As a panel you should have an agreed approach to shaking hands with candidates. It is disorientating for the candidate if one panel member stands to shake hands when they enter the room, while the others remain seated. If your agreed approach is to shake hands, then this should happen as the chairperson introduces the panel members when the candidate enters the room, before they are invited to sit down.

Once the candidate is seated the chairperson should:

- Thank the candidate for coming.
- Check they have switched off their cell phone.
- Outline the interview process—how long it will last and the order in which the panel members will be asking their questions.
- Reassure the candidate that the questions will all be related to the criteria covered in the person specification.
- Let them know that notes will be taken to provide a record of the interview.
- Invite them to have a drink of water if they wish.

Rapport Building

All of the above steps will help put a candidate at ease and, if done in a welcoming way with the appropriate tone, start building rapport between the panel and the candidate.

Some specific steps that panel members can take to build rapport are:

- Making eye contact with the candidate.
- Smiling at the candidate.
- Looking interested when the candidate is talking to you.
- Using appropriate body language, such as adopting an open posture (i.e., not sitting hunched up with your arms folded).
- Avoiding annoying personal habits (e.g., clicking a pen or rocking on your chair).

Sometimes these points are outside of our awareness. For this reason, while it is sometimes an uncomfortable experience, it is beneficial to see yourself on video. Perhaps you could create an opportunity to do this—for example, if you have a team member who would benefit from practice as an interviewee you could hold a "mock" interview for them and video it. You could then provide feedback to each other and watch the video to identify learning points for yourselves. When people do this they often identify nonverbal and verbal habits that they were previously unaware of—aspects of their body language that may get in the way of building rapport with candidates, or verbal patterns that may become irritating, such as excessive "ums" or repeated use of words such as "Right" and "Okay."

Keeping the Interview On Track

However good your preparation has been there may still be times when an interview seems to drift off track. The candidate is talking, but they do not seem to be providing the evidence you need to assess their ability to do the job. This can happen for many reasons, some to do with the candidate and some to do with the interviewer. These are set out in Table 6.1.

Table 6.1 Reasons why the interview may go off track

Interviewer's responsibility	Candidate's responsibility
Lack of rapport building	Not listening closely enough to the question
Unclear or poorly phrased questions	Not understanding the question
Questions not sufficiently related to the specified criteria	Not wanting to answer the question
Understanding not demonstrated through the use of skills such as summarizing and reflecting	Long, vague, rambling answers
Inability to intervene and get the candidate back on track	Wanting to divert the interview on to their own agenda (and away from that of the panel)
Attention drifts	Attention drifts

In order to keep the interview on track you need two sets of skills—firstly, the skills to minimize the risk of drifting off track in the first place, and secondly, the skills to intervene effectively and bring the interview back on track if it happens.

The way that an interviewer can keep both their questioning and the candidate's answers closely focused on the relevant criteria is by following the four steps of the Interviewing Skills Flow Chart.

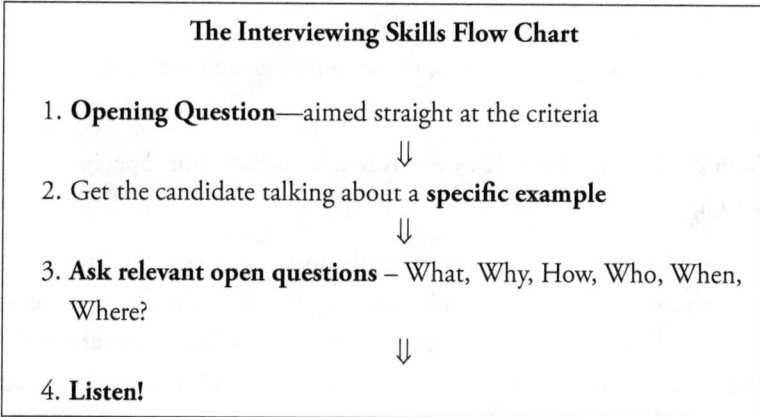

The Interviewing Skills Flow Chart

1. **Opening Question**—aimed straight at the criteria

⇓

2. Get the candidate talking about a **specific example**

⇓

3. **Ask relevant open questions** – What, Why, How, Who, When, Where?

⇓

4. **Listen!**

Following these four steps is the key to your success as an interviewer—so let's look at each of them in more detail.

Step 1—Ask an Open-Ended Question That Is Directly Relevant to the Criteria

A great way to do this is to use *TED* questions:

- Tell
- Explain
- Describe

The following are examples of how you can ask TED questions that are directly aimed at the interview criteria:

*One of the attributes we're looking for is the ability to resolve problems for a customer when things go wrong. **Tell me** about a time when you've done that.*

*You mention on your application form that you maintained performance in priority areas when your team was under pressure. **Explain** to me how you did that.*

*You state on your application form that you managed a poor performer whom you brought up to the required standard. **Describe** how you went about doing that.*

These questions point the candidate in the right direction, by being clear and specific about the type of examples you are looking for.

Step 2—Ensure That They Answer with a Relevant, Specific Example

Asking for a relevant, specific example does not necessarily mean you will get one! People often find it easier to generalize—it is what we tend to do in day-to-day speech. You may also find candidates who are confident in their ability to sound impressive when generalizing, but fear being exposed if they have to talk in depth about a specific example from their experience.

The following phrases are sure signs that a candidate is **NOT** providing you with a specific example...

*What I **always** say is ...*
*What I **would do** is ...*
*The way **we** deal with that is to ...*

Notice that these phrases use either the present tense ("What I always say is ...") or the future tense ("What I would do is ..."). If a candidate talks in the present tense they are generalizing, and if they talk in the future tense their answers will be hypothetical. A candidate needs to talk in the *past tense* if they are to provide you with the specific, detailed evidence you need.

If you hear a candidate using these words and phrases you need to be prepared to assertively intervene at an early stage in order to redirect them back to the criteria (see below—"Assertive Interruptions").

You should also listen carefully for use of the word "we" instead of "I." Given that many tasks involve working as part of a team it is sometimes genuinely difficult for a candidate to identify their part in what was done. However, you are not interviewing them as a representative of their team—you are interviewing them as an individual candidate. You therefore need to get the candidate to be specific about their personal contribution to any team activity, for example, by saying:

> You say that "we" decided to take that course of action—what was your personal contribution to that decision-making process?

Step 3—Once They Are Talking About a Relevant, Specific Example—Ask Them Questions About It!

As we have already seen, it can be hard work focusing a candidate in order to generate the kind of detailed evidence you are looking for—so once you've got them talking about a relevant example make sure that you milk it for all the evidence you can! A good example will be like a wet sponge dripping with evidence, and your job as an interviewer is to wring out that soggy sponge so by the end of the interview you have a bucket full of evidence. In order to do this remember Kipling's *Six Honest Serving Men*:

> I keep six honest serving men (They taught me all I knew);
> Their names are What and Why and When and How and Where and Who

Step 4—Listen!

This may sound obvious, but actually doing it is often harder than you think. What *should* happen in an interview is that you ask a question, then listen intently to the candidate's answer. But what often happens is that once the candidate starts answering a question, the interviewer immediately starts thinking about what to ask next. This means that when the candidate stops talking the interviewer doesn't have a clue as to what they have just been told, and their next question may not make sense to the candidate at all. Even worse, you may ask them something they have just told you!

There are three steps involved in listening to and making sense of the candidate's answers:

1. *Listen carefully* to what the candidate says. This involves focusing and giving them your *full attention*—not allowing yourself to be distracted by anything else that's going on—including what you might ask next.
2. *Make sense* of what they have said. If they have given a lengthy answer a useful technique is to *paraphrase it*—state the key points back to them, for example:

So you heard shouting, went out to the office and two team members were squaring up to each other.

Paraphrasing has benefits for everyone involved in the interview:

- It enables *you* to make sense of what the candidate has said to you.
- It demonstrates to *the candidate* that you have understood— or gives them a chance to correct any errors or misunderstandings.
- It gives your *note taker* a chance to catch up!

3. *Formulate your next question.* With practice you will find that this starts to flow naturally from your paraphrasing. For example:

So you heard shouting, went out to the office and two team members were squaring up to each other—what did you do?

Assertive Interruptions

Sometimes candidates talk generally or hypothetically at some length because the interviewer feels unable to interrupt them. Many of us are brought up believing that it is rude to interrupt, or lack the self-confidence to do so. However, the result of this in an interview is that the precious and limited time available for generating evidence ends up being frittered away on generalities. This is not in anyone's best interests—the panel or the candidate.

You therefore have a responsibility to interrupt and refocus a candidate if they are not providing the evidence you need. This can be difficult to do, particularly if a candidate is in full flow and it seems hard to get a word in edgeways. For this reason interviewers need to practice and develop the skill of assertive interruption.

To assertively interrupt a candidate you first need to adopt the appropriate body language. Lean forward and raise your hand—like a cop stopping traffic. As you do this say:

Let me stop you there ...

Usually a candidate will respond to this and stop talking. If they fail to respond raise your hand again and say:

I need you to stop for a moment ...

Once the candidate has stopped talking and given you their attention then redirect them to the avenue you wish them to go down—again like a police officer directing traffic! If possible do this by recognizing and building upon something they have said which was of value. For example:

Let me stop you there ... I was interested when you mentioned that the argument was overheard by the customers who were waiting in reception. What did you do about that aspect of it?

If it is not possible to do this you may need simply to provide the candidate with very clear clarification of what you are looking for. For example:

You've been talking about an argument between two of your colleagues, but I'm interested in your Customer Relations skills. Tell me about a situation which directly involved you dealing with a customer.

Sometimes a candidate may go off track because your line of questioning was not sufficiently clear to begin with. If this is the case then be honest about it:

> *I'm sorry—perhaps my question wasn't sufficiently clear. What I'm interested in is how you dealt with a situation directly involving your customers, not one involving your colleagues.*

Whichever of these approaches you use, it is essential that you develop the ability to politely but firmly interrupt—and if you are not getting the evidence you need, it is in the candidate's best interests for you to do so.

Some Pitfalls and How to Overcome Them

In this section I will identify some of the pitfalls that can arise during the interview, what you can do to overcome them or—ideally—to minimize the risk of them arising in the first place.

1. *Paying too much attention to first impressions*

Read any guide to being a successful interviewee and it will tell you that it is vital to make a good first impression. Why? Because it's true! First impressions count, and studies suggest that the first few minutes of an interview are crucial in deciding whether or not a candidate will be offered a job.

A candidate may make a positive first impression by dressing smartly, smiling at you, using assertive body language, and speaking in a clear, authoritative tone of voice. First impressions are particularly powerful if they may remind us of how we would like to see ourselves!

We have already discussed the "Halo effect," when interviewers immediately feel that this is the "right type of person," leading to them spending the rest of the interview seeking evidence to confirm that initial judgment, rather than objectively seeking evidence of the candidate's ability to fully meet the specified criteria.

We have also discussed the "Horns effect," where a candidate makes such a poor first impression that you mentally attach a pair of devilish horns to the sides of their head! Again the risk is that once panel members have formed this initial judgment they spend the rest of the interview trying to prove themselves right.

As an interviewer it is important that you guard against attaching too much weight to your first impressions. The candidate who makes a great first impression may turn out to be superficial and shallow, and the candidate who makes a terrible first impression may simply have been nervous or not able to afford to buy a smart suit. To get a full picture of a candidate's abilities you need to pay full attention to the evidence generated throughout the whole of the interview.

2. Prejudices and stereotyping

This pitfall is closely related to the Halo and Horns effects, which often arise because of prejudices and stereotypes held on the part of panel members. The chairperson should remind panel members of their responsibilities in relation to both the law and their organization's equal opportunities policies.

However, the risk of unfair discrimination arising from prejudices and stereotyping is wider than this. I remember chairing an interview where one of the panel members said in the assessment discussion that she would not employ a candidate who had chewed gum during the interview. I replied that that this was not part of our stated assessment criteria, but the panel member was insistent that the candidate had behaved inappropriately in the interview and should be marked down for this.

In the subsequent feedback discussion with the candidate (who was passed by the panel overall) I mentioned this issue. The candidate told me that she got very nervous during interviews, and chewing gum was the only way to stop her mouth from becoming completely dry. If we had acted upon the panel member's prejudice against her for chewing gum during the interview we would have failed a strong candidate, who went on to do a great job.

The chairperson should remind panel members that all candidates must be judged on merit, against the specified assessment criteria.

3. The candidate who takes control of the interview

Some candidates will have their own agenda for the interview and will attempt to stick to this, no matter what you might ask them. It's like listening to a politician being interviewed, when they ignore the questions and say whatever they want to say.

The problem with this type of candidate is that what they want to talk about may not match what you need to find out about. The interview can then degenerate into a battle for control, which can end in frustration for everyone involved.

It is important to use your assertive interruption skills with this type of candidate, and to be quite explicit about why you are asking particular questions. For example:

One of the key responsibilities for this job is managing a budget of $3.5 million. I need you to demonstrate that you have the experience and skills to manage that kind of budget.

Under no circumstances should you give up and allow control to pass to the candidate. If they do not respond to your first assertive interruption then keep doing it until they do. Remember that you and your colleagues are likely to be much clearer about the key requirements for the job than the candidate, and it is therefore your responsibility to point the candidate in the right direction.

If a candidate repeatedly fails to respond to your efforts to point them in the right direction, then that becomes their responsibility. Their failure to answer your questions should be recorded in your notes of the interview, and should be addressed explicitly with the candidate if feedback is provided following the interview.

4. *The candidate who goes quiet*

This is the opposite of the last example, but can be equally difficult to handle. It is a powerful skill for an interviewer to be able to live with silence, but if it feels like it will never end it can be disconcerting for everyone involved.

If your question is initially met with silence it may simply mean that the candidate is thinking about what they want to say. Intervening too early may interrupt their thought processes, and have an adverse effect on their answer.

Watch the candidate's body language. According to the theory of Neuro Linguistic Programming, if their eyes move upwards and to the right it may mean that they are trying to visualize a situation as it happened. If they are looking downwards it may mean that they are trying to recall how they felt, but if it is accompanied by fidgeting of the hands, legs, and feet, it may indicate that they are feeling anxious and struggling to come up with an answer. So in the first instance you should give them a few moments' thinking time, whereas in the second you may need to intervene.

Interventions may be on a content level or on a process level. Examples of *content level* interventions would be:

Would you like me to repeat the question?

or

Do you need me to clarify the question?

Examples of *process level* interventions may be:

Take a few moments if you need to ...

or

You've gone very quiet—do we need to take a break for a few moments?

5. *The candidate who becomes upset*

On rare occasions a candidate going quiet is the first signal that they are becoming upset or distressed.

If a candidate is showing signs of distress the chairperson should offer to "pause" the interview to give them time to gather themselves. Remind them that there is water available if they would like some. Offer them the opportunity to leave the room for five minutes before restarting the interview—but also remember that this can only be five minutes—there are other candidates waiting and it would be unfair to delay their interviews.

It should be the candidate's choice whether to restart or to abandon the interview. If they do not wish to continue it may be appropriate to ask one of your staff to sit with them for a while before they leave. You may also wish to phone them later to check that they are okay.

Remember that if a candidate becomes upset it is unlikely to have been your fault. Many people find interviews to be stressful experiences, and this is likely to be exacerbated if they are experiencing other difficulties in their lives. As panel members you need to respond to the situation professionally, and balance your duty of care to that individual with your responsibility to maintain a fair process for the other candidates.

6. *The panel member who overruns*

As discussed in Chapter 5, the chairperson has overall responsibility for ensuring that the interview runs to time, but good timekeeping is a collective responsibility of the whole panel. Each panel member should be aware of time so that they can cover their allotted criteria before the chair gives the signal for them to draw their questions to a close.

Some panel members are better at meeting this responsibility than others! There are a number of reasons why panel members sometimes fail to respond to the chairperson's time signal—they may be so engrossed in discussion with the candidate that they miss it, or so sure that they are generating quality evidence that they choose to ignore it.

If the initial time signal fails to get a response the chair should repeat the signal. If it is ignored for a second time the chairperson needs to make a polite but firm intervention, along the lines of:

Sorry to interrupt, but we need to draw this part of the interview to a close now.

After the interview, the chairperson should remind the panel member of their responsibility to keep to the agreed timings.

Closing the Interview

Before closing the interview the chairperson should check whether the panel members have any remaining questions they wish to ask. This provides a final opportunity to address any gaps which may be remaining from the discussion during the interview.

It is the chairperson's overall responsibility to check that all of the criteria have been fully tested during the interview. It is a good idea for the chairperson to have a fresh copy of the person specification in front of them for each interview. He or she can then tick off the criteria when satisfied that it has been fully tested, and note any follow-up questions to ask at the end of the interview.

Once the panel have asked all their questions the chairperson should give the candidate an opportunity to ask any questions. These should be answered fully but as succinctly as possible. You may find it helpful to anticipate likely questions and ensure that you have the answers—typical questions may be as basic as how to claim travel expenses, or related to issues such as where the post will be located and lines of responsibility. Do not get drawn into a fresh area of discussion with a candidate when you are bringing the interview to a close.

Let the candidate know when and how (i.e., by phone, e-mail, or letter) they will be hearing from you. Thank them for attending the interview and show them out of the room. Make sure that you have agreed who will do this in advance—it's another stage with the potential for unnecessary awkward moments!

Summary of Chapter 6—Conducting the Interview: The Process

In this chapter I have covered:

- *The importance of starting the interview on the right note*, by making sure that the necessary practical arrangements run smoothly and by building rapport with the candidate once they enter the room.
- *The need to keep the interview on track*—by following the interviewing skills flow chart and, if necessary, using the technique of "Assertive Interruption."
- *The importance of fully testing the criteria.* This involves each panel member keeping to the interview plan. The chair of the panel has overall responsibility for ensuring that all aspects of the criteria have been fully tested before the candidate leaves the room.
- *Six potential pitfalls*—how to minimize the risk of them arising in the first place and how to manage them if they do.
- *How to close the interview.*

CHAPTER 7

Conducting the Interview: Five Key Skills

This chapter focuses on the following essential skills:

- *Conversation management*—the ability to manage the interview in order to gather the information you need.
- *Questioning skills*—to enable you to obtain detailed evidence of the candidate's abilities.
- *Listening skills*—to enable you to quickly identify where the candidate is providing the information you need, and where you need to ask further questions.
- *Note-taking skills*—to enable you to record the candidate's answers so that you can assess them fully following the interview.
- *Analytical skills*—to enable you to assess candidates against the criteria set out in the person specification, at both the sift and interview stages.

Conversation Management

Conversation management is not about *what* you ask, but *how* you ask it. It is about managing the interview in such a way that the candidate will feel sufficiently at ease to answer your questions openly and honestly.

Conversation management is used by investigative agencies, such as the police. Of course there are major differences between a recruitment interview and an interview being carried out as part of a police investigation, but there are also similarities. Recruitment candidates often feel high levels of stress and anxiety, particularly if they really want the job. Using techniques to build rapport will help to overcome this. At the same time some candidates may also have information that they do not wish to reveal, perhaps some shortcomings in some of the areas they know will be tested. By using conversation management techniques you are more likely to conduct an interview where these are revealed.

Conversation management has three core elements:

1. *Reciprocity*

Reciprocity is the basis of all human social exchanges. Put simply, if we receive something from another person we are likely to reciprocate by giving something back. This is particularly the case if there is an alignment between what we say and an indication of the emotion that goes with it. So if you say "Good morning" and smile at someone, they are likely to reciprocate with a similar response and smile back. In an interview this is the first stage of building rapport with the interviewee.

2. *Rapport*

Building rapport will put the candidate at ease, making them feel comfortable to answer your questions. It may also lead them to let their guard down, and talk more openly about situations that did not go so well.

You can build rapport by

- Showing Respect to the candidate. This can be demonstrated by your behavior towards them, which should be courteous, warm, sincere, and attentive.
- Demonstrating *Empathy*—the ability to see things from another person's point of view, sometimes described as "stepping into their shoes." This can be difficult to achieve; for example, if you feel that a candidate has dealt with a situation poorly, it may be evident from your facial expression or tone of voice. The candidate is likely to notice this, and may refrain from giving you any more information about what happened, or give you a distorted account which shows them

in a better light. For this reason it is important to suspend judgment until after the interview is finished, and maintain a positive, empathetic approach while they are giving their account.

- Being *supportive* of the candidate. This may involve behaviors such as reassuring them it is okay to take time to think before answering, or by assisting recall, for example, prompting them with situations from their application form. However, it is also important to avoid being excessively supportive. Overuse of reassuring behaviors might give the candidate the impression that you are being patronizing, while overenthusiastic responses to their answers might give the misleading impression that they have got the job!
- Using *straightforward language*, which the candidate is able to understand easily. Avoid use of jargon or "in-house" language—while it may be familiar to you and your fellow panel members, it may be mystifying to the candidate. It is also important to keep your questions short and simple—the longer the questions, the more confusing they are likely to be to the interviewee.

3. *Sequencing*

Your interview should follow a structured sequence, ensuring that you gather the information you need to ascertain the candidate's suitability for the job. Achieving this involves:

- Preparing an interview plan before the interview.
- Applying the plan during the interview.
- Making interventions to refocus on the plan if the interview is digressing from it.

In order to ensure fairness each interview should follow the same structure. For example, it would not be fair to ease some candidates into their interviews by beginning with strengths-based questions, whereas for others you begin by asking challenging behavior description questions.

Questioning Skills

In day-to-day life we ask many different types of questions, without any need to analyze them or their effects. When preparing to conduct an interview it is necessary to bring these subconscious skills into our awareness, so that we can consciously use the types of questions that will be most productive in obtaining the evidence we need from the candidate.

In this section I will consider the following question types, identifying which are likely to be productive in interviews and how they can be effectively deployed:

- Open-ended questions
- Open probing questions
- Hypothetical questions
- Closed questions
- Limiting questions
- Leading questions
- Multiple questions

Open-Ended Questions

Open-ended questions are a key part of recruitment interviewing. They are designed to encourage the interviewee to recall a critical incident in detail, enabling them to open up and provide a full and thorough answer. They also allow the interviewee to control the flow of information.

As discussed in Chapter 6, open-ended questions will often follow the TED approach, beginning with the phrase "Tell me," or the words "Explain," or "Describe." A skillful interviewer will precede the question by linking it to the relevant criteria or a situation described by the candidate on their application form. For example:

*One of the attributes we're looking for here is the ability to resolve problems for a customer when things go wrong. **Tell** me about a time when you've done that.*

Once you have asked an open-ended question it is important to shift into listening mode (see below). Research shows that the most reliable and detailed answers are secured from asking open-ended questions. Ideally you should listen until the interviewee has finished answering, at which point you may investigate key points of the answer in more detail by asking open probing questions.

One of the risks of asking open-ended questions is receiving open-ended answers, which may be very lengthy and stray from the point. If this is the case you may need to intervene and gently redirect the candidate, or use the assertive interruption technique discussed in Chapter 6.

Open Probing Questions

These questions are the Kipling's "Six Honest Serving Men," discussed in Chapter 6. Open probing questions begin with:

- What
- Why
- When
- How
- Where
- Who

These questions can be used to generate more detailed information about a particular situation than the candidate may have provided in their response to your initial open-ended question. Remember that some answers that initially sound impressive may not stand up to scrutiny—there may be areas that the candidate has chosen to "gloss over," or details they may have missed out. It is therefore important to always ask probing follow-up questions as set out below.

"What" questions establish and clarify points of information, for example:

What was the first thing you did?

They can be used to probe the candidate's thinking, for example:

What were you thinking at that moment?

"What" questions can also generate important evidence by establishing details of dialogue, for example:

You said you were angry with your colleague—what precisely did you say to her?

"Why" questions establish the reasoning behind the candidate's actions, for example:

Why did you decide to do that?

Be careful with your tone when asking "why" questions—with the wrong tone of voice or body language they can come across as interrogatory or accusing. You can sometimes soften the tone by changing a "why" question into a "what" question—for example:

What made you decide to do that?

"When" questions enable you to establish the sequence of events, for example:

When did you talk to your staff member about this?

When exactly did you get back to the customer?

"How" questions can be used to establish the processes followed by the candidate, for example:

How did you go about doing that?

As with many probing questions it can be helpful to link it to the candidate's previous answer, for example:

You say that you tackled the team member about his persistent lateness—tell me in detail how you went about doing that?

"Where" questions not only provide information about the location of events, but can also provide important indications about the candidate's judgment, for example:

So you talked to the team member about his persistent lateness— **where** *did that discussion take place?*

"Who" questions provide information about who was involved in particular events, for example:

Who *was involved in that discussion?*

Once again they can also be used to test the candidate's judgment, for example:

Who *did you consult before making that decision?*

Note that all the open-ended and probing questions illustrated here are in the *past tense*. If you stray into the present tense the candidate will generalize instead of talking about specific examples. This is fine if you are using the Model Answer-Based Interviewing technique, but when using Behavior Description Interviewing you should ensure your questions are in the past tense.

You may also have noticed that some of these probing questions include the words "precisely," "in detail," and "exactly." This is the PIE approach to questioning, used to pin an interviewee down to providing detailed information in their answers:

What **precisely** *did you say to them?*

Tell me **in detail** *how you did that ...*

What **exactly** *did you do then?*

Hypothetical Questions

Hypothetical questions may sound similar to those already covered, but while the open-ended and open probing questions involve getting the candidate to talk about what they *actually did* in a specific situation, and hypothetical questions ask what they *would do* if they were faced with a particular situation. For example:

> What **would** you do if you heard a team member having an argument with a customer?
> How **would** you handle the situation if you had a team member who persistently arrived late?

You would ask hypothetical questions such as these if you were applying Model Answer Interviewing. It is fine to use Model Answer-Based Interviewing as part of a blended interview, but it should not be used in isolation from other interviewing techniques. There are two main reasons for this.

One is implicit in the name of the technique—Model Answer-Based Interviewing. An intelligent candidate will anticipate your questions and come prepared with a stock of model answers! While these may sound very impressive they may not be an accurate guide to what that candidate would actually do if faced with the situation in practice.

The second reason to use hypothetical questions with care is that they generate hypothetical answers—which may lack the depth, richness, and complexity of real-life examples. For this reason you should ask about specific examples where possible, using hypothetical questions to plug the gaps.

Closed Questions

A closed question is one that can be answered "yes" or "no." For example:

> **Did** you do that?
> **Was** that your idea?

Generally speaking, closed questions are not encouraged in recruitment interviewing. One reason for this is that they encourage short—often "Yes" or "No"—answers, when what the interviewer should be doing is encouraging the candidate to open up and provide detailed evidence of their capabilities. There is the additional risk that the "right" answer is implicit in the question—if a candidate has just described an idea that worked well their answer to the question "Was that your idea?" is likely to be yes!

Occasionally it will be appropriate to use a closed question in order to quickly establish the facts of what happened, particularly if you have a candidate who is verbose and has difficulty keeping to the point. In these circumstances you might clarify the information provided and draw the example to a close by asking clarifying questions such as

Is that what you decided to do?
Was that what you actually did?

Limiting Questions

Limiting questions give the interviewee a controlled choice of answers. They might be used to clarify information given by the candidate, or to confirm the sequence of events. For example:

So who did you speak to first—the customer or your colleague?
So what was your priority—meeting the new target or clearing the work arrears?

The risk with using limiting questions is that none of the options you offer may match with what the candidate actually did. This may prevent you from obtaining a full and accurate picture of the situation the candidate has been describing.

Leading Questions

If limiting questions are to be used with caution, leading questions should not be used at all! However, they sometimes "slip into" an interview, particularly when the interviewer is keen to confirm the impression they have already gained of a candidate rather than gathering further information. For example:

Would you say that your decision was a good one?

A candidate will almost certainly answer yes, unless there is already clear evidence to the contrary.

I guess you learnt a lot from that experience, didn't you?

Again it will be clear to the candidate that the "right" answer to this question is "Yes"!

Multiple Questions

Interviewers do not usually intend to ask multiple questions, but they arise when the interviewer is trying to take in a lot of information and is uncertain of which line of questioning to pursue next. This can result in a series of questions all coming out together, for example:

So your team member had this big argument with the customer— what did you say to him? Who did you speak to first—your team member or the customer? And how did you calm things down? It must have had an effect on everyone else in the waiting area—what did you do about that?

These are all potentially productive lines of questioning, but they need separating if you are to be successful in obtaining detailed evidence of what the candidate did. When multiple questions are asked candidates will often only answer one part—often the part that shows them in the best light!

Listening Skills

In a recruitment interview around 80 percent of the talking should be done by the interviewee. While this is taking place the main responsibility of the panel members is to listen.

The problem with this is that each panel member will have other things going in their mind which interfere with their ability to listen effectively. The chairperson will be monitoring progress of the interview, and noting down areas for follow-up questions at the end. The panel member who is not leading the questioning at this stage of the interview will be taking notes. It may seem surprising that note taking is not conducive to effective listening, but the focus of the note taker's attention will be on simply recording what is being said, not interpreting or making sense of it. Meanwhile the final panel member, who is leading the questioning, may be too focused on thinking about what they will ask next to listen properly to the candidate's answers!

All of these factors lead to *superficial listening*. The panel members will be aware that they have a responsibility to appear as though they are listening. They will therefore adopt appropriate body language, such as looking at the candidate, and perhaps sometimes nodding to demonstrate understanding. They may support this with verbal signals such as "mmm" or neutral terms, such as "I see." It may therefore appear to the candidate that the panel are listening attentively, but in reality they are going through the motions and, most crucially, not taking everything in.

It is clear from this that questioning skills alone are not enough. There is no value in asking detailed questions that probe and investigate specific incidents unless one or more of the panel members is engaged in listening intently to the answers. They need to *listen actively*. This has five main aspects:

1. *Ask open questions*

As I have already identified, asking the right question at the right time is a key skill for an interviewer. Asking open questions is the first stage in encouraging someone to talk openly to you.

2. *Summarize*

This helps to show that you've listened to, and understood, what's been said. As discussed in relation to the interview skills flowchart in Chapter 6, an accurate summary helps everyone involved in the interview:

The Candidate—because it demonstrates that you're listening and understanding their main points.

Yourself—because it enables you to pause and make sense of what the candidate has said before you formulate your next question.

The Chairperson—because it helps them to identify which criteria have been covered, and where there might be gaps to address with follow-up questions at the end.

The Note Taker—because it gives them a chance to catch up!

3. Reflect

Summarizing demonstrates your understanding of the *content* of a candidate's answer, whereas *reflecting* demonstrates your understanding of how they might have been *feeling*. Demonstrating this deeper level of understanding will encourage a candidate to tell you more. You can do this by using a phrase or even just a single word that demonstrates your ability to empathize with how the candidate seems to be feeling about the situation they are describing, for example:

That sounds very stressful ...

Sometimes a single word will do:

Challenging ...

If done accurately your reflection will help recapture the emotion that the candidate felt in the moment, which will enable them to recall what happened and talk about it in detail.

4. Clarify

There may be aspects of their examples that candidates wish to skirt around or gloss over. This may be for a variety of reasons—it may be an emotionally charged situation that they still find difficult to talk about, or they may not feel completely happy with the way they handled some aspects of it.

Getting a candidate to talk more fully about these aspects of their experience will provide you with telling evidence of their ability to perform effectively in challenging situations. You may need to clarify what happened by using open-ended questions and phrases such as:

Tell me more about ...
What exactly happened when ...
I was interested that you mentioned ...

5. React

As a panel member you don't have to remain completely neutral in your reactions to the candidate. We have already identified the benefits of building rapport and showing empathy with the candidate. If they tell you about a stressful or emotionally challenging situation it is appropriate to react by empathizing with them, and at the end by thanking them for telling you about it.

That sounds like it must have been really difficult. Thank you for talking about it so openly.

By following these steps you will encourage the candidate to go on talking, and providing you with evidence of their ability to do the job.

Note-Taking Skills

In many organizations the only record of what is said during an interview is the notes taken by the panel members. It is therefore vital that panel members are able to take notes which provide a thorough record of both:
The questions asked

- To ensure that all the interview criteria have been fully covered.
- To provide a record of questions asked in case of appeal by the candidate—for example, if they complain that questions asked were discriminatory or unfair.

And:
The answers given

- To ensure that there is a full and accurate record of answers given by the candidate.
- To provide information for the assessment process following the interview.
- To provide a record of answers given in case of appeal by the candidate.

Effective note taking is both important and difficult to do, but despite this, it is often neglected when interviewers are being trained or interviews are being prepared. When planning the interview it is essential to:

- Allocate roles—so that no-one will be expected to lead the questioning and take notes at the same time, and that it is clear who is responsible for note taking at each stage of the interview.
- Draw up interview record sheets. These may be adapted from the interview preparation sheets you have already prepared. Opening questions can be recorded on these in advance, reducing the amount of note taking required during the interview. These will also ensure that notes are taken in the same format in all interviews, making it easier to compare the evidence provided by candidates.

An example of an interview record sheet can be found at Appendix 9.

When taking notes it is particularly important to record the parts of the candidates' answers that relate directly to the criteria being tested. Other aspects, such as background detail or setting the context for an example, can be summarized.

It is also acceptable to summarize the questions in your notes. If the panel member leading the questioning summarizes an answer before leading into a question about what happened next it is acceptable to write:

Summary—what next?

A question such as "Why did you take that decision?" may be abbreviated to

Decision—why?

When taking notes of both questions and answers it is acceptable to use abbreviations and acronyms, as long as they will be understandable to your fellow panel members and anyone else who has to look at the notes afterwards.

As with most skills, note taking becomes easier with practice. If possible it is good preparation to sit in on some interviews before you conduct them as a panel member. This is an opportunity to practice your note taking and compare them with those taken by the members of the panel.

Analytical Skills

The skills considered so far in this chapter are the ones you need to use to gather and record evidence during an interview. Once the interview has finished you need to *analyze* the evidence you have gathered to identify:

- Where the evidence presented by the candidate meets the specified criteria.
- Where the evidence presented by the candidate fails to meet the specified criteria.
- Which of the candidates has demonstrated meeting the criteria most fully.

However, this is not the first point in the process where you need good analytical skills. They are needed throughout the recruitment process at the following stages:

- Analyzing the requirements of the job, in order to draw up an accurate job description.
- Analyzing the knowledge, experience, skills, and attributes required in order to do the job effectively, so that these can be set out in the person specification.
- Analyzing the evidence presented on the application forms at the sifting stage, in order to identify which candidates to invite for interview.

There are many definitions of analytical skills. Most include the following components:

- The ability to solve problems.

- The ability to weigh up a range of sources of evidence—which may conflict with one another.
- The ability to make logical decisions based on the available evidence.

The stages at which you need to analyze the evidence presented by job applicants are:

1. The sift
2. Following the interview

At both of these stages the criteria against which you are analyzing the candidate's evidence will be the same, that is, how fully he or she meets the requirements of the person specification. What will be different is the standard the candidate needs to achieve. At the sift you want to be satisfied whether there is sufficient evidence in the application form of the candidate's ability to meet the criteria to justify inviting him or her to interview. At the interview stage you will gather further evidence to enable you to make your final decision as to which of the applicants is the best person for the job.

At both stages analyzing the evidence presented by the applicant involves considering it carefully against the requirements of the person specification. Table 7.1 sets out what constitutes good evidence, and what might be considered poor evidence.

Table 7.1 Good quality evidence versus poor quality evidence

Good Quality Evidence	Poor Quality Evidence
Answers that are directly relevant to the specified criteria.	Answers only vaguely relate to the specified criteria.
Specific examples of what the applicant has actually done.	General statements—non-specific and vague.
Explanations of the reasoning behind what the applicant did.	No clear explanation for applicant's actions.
Outcomes—positive results achieved as a result of what the applicant did.	No evidence of what was achieved—or evidence of negative outcomes.
Examples that are clearly attributable to the applicant (i.e., based on their own actions and decisions).	Examples that may be attributable to the actions and decisions of others.

In addition to being clear about what constitutes good and poor quality evidence you will need to be able to apply a rating scale in order to score each applicant for each of the criteria. An example rating scale and rating forms are included in *Chapter 2—Laying the Foundations*. A blank panel member rating form can be found at Appendix 4, and a blank panel rating form can be found at Appendix 5.

Chapter 8—After the Interview—will look in more detail at applying your analytical skills at this stage of the process.

Summary of Chapter 7—Conducting the Interview: Five Key Skills

In this chapter I have explored five key skills:

- Conversation management
- Questioning skills
- Listening skills
- Note taking skills
- Analytical skills

These skills are the essential tools you will need to be an effective member of an interview panel.

Conversation management is the set of skills which enables you to manage the interview effectively. The three key elements are reciprocity, rapport, and sequencing.

Questioning skills will enable you to gather the information that you need about a candidate at interview. Begin by asking open-ended questions, to encourage candidates to talk about specific examples. Then follow up with open probing questions, to find out in detail about what they did and why they did it.

Active listening skills will show candidates that you are interested in what they have to say, and enable you to understand and interpret their evidence as it is being presented. This will enable you to make sound decisions about which areas to probe further.

Effective note taking will enable you to make an accurate record of the key points of the interview, which will then form the basis of the assessment process following the interview.

Analytical skills are essential throughout the recruitment process, particularly when assessing evidence presented by applicants.

CHAPTER 8

After the Interview

This chapter provides a structured process for assessing evidence and selecting the right candidate, and sets out the steps required to complete the selection process. It covers:

- What to do when the candidate leaves the room.
- A structured process for assessing evidence and reaching agreement as a panel.
- Ensuring that you select the right candidate.
- Notification of successful and unsuccessful candidates.
- Requesting references for successful candidates.
- Giving feedback to unsuccessful candidates.

When the Candidate Leaves the Room

Stay quiet! There are two reasons for this. Firstly, the candidate may still be in the corridor outside and able to hear what you say. An injudicious remark that is overheard by him or her, even though the interview has finished, could result in a complaint or appeal against the result of the interview. At the very least it will undermine the professionalism with which you have conducted the process up to that point.

Secondly, a comment at this stage will undermine the integrity of the assessment process. As with the sift stage each panel member should come to their initial assessment independently. Premature comments about the candidate are a barrier to this taking place.

The panel should follow a *structured process* for assessing evidence and reaching agreement. This involves three stages:

Stage 1—each panel member reviews the evidence and comes to his or her individual assessment for each of the criteria.

Stage 2—the panel share and discuss their ratings for each of the criteria.

Stage 3—the panel agree and record their ratings for each of the criteria and their overall rating.

I will now look at each of these stages in more detail.

Stage 1—Individual Assessments

Each member of the panel should have a blank panel member rating form. They should work through the criteria listed, noting their initial ratings and brief reasons for the ratings. Although there should be no discussion, *it is essential that panel members look at the notes of the whole interview*—either by swapping the notes between them or by making a quick copy. This is for two reasons:

1. Human memory is fallible, and what you think you recall from a particular stage of the interview may differ from what was actually said. Notes taken at the time are more likely to be accurate than your recollections.
2. As highlighted in earlier chapters, the criteria will often overlap with each other. For example, you may feel that there is a gap in the evidence provided by the candidate when they were talking about Customer Relations. However, if they talked about another example relating to customer service when discussing Communicating Effectively, their answers might have included evidence that addressed this original gap. It is therefore important to consider all of the evidence before you reach your conclusions.

When considering the evidence presented by the candidate it is useful to apply the *RAILS* acronym:

R—Relevance. Has the candidate provided you with answers which were relevant to the questions you asked, and which gives you relevant evidence of their ability to do the job they have applied for?

A—Attributable. Is the evidence clearly attributable to the candidate? As already discussed, candidates often use the word "We," particularly when talking about activities undertaken as part of a team. Have they been able to identify their specific contribution to those activities?

I—Indicative. Is the evidence the candidate has presented indicative of their general performance? Some candidates have only one or two good examples, which they go back to time and time again throughout the interview. This may be a sign that the candidate has limited evidence of their ability to do the job. During the interview you might have addressed this by specifically asking the candidate to talk about a different example. Were they able to do this? If they did, was the evidence they presented of a suitable standard?

L—Level. Does the level of evidence presented by the candidate match the level of the vacancy you are looking to fill? If you are recruiting for a leadership role, one of your selection criteria may be the ability to make good, fully considered, decisions. These may have an impact on other people, finances, or your organization's strategy. If the candidate provided examples of decisions which only affected themselves, with no financial or strategic implications, they have not provided evidence at the right level.

S—Specific. Has the candidate provided specific examples, particular occasions when they have been able to demonstrate their strengths, or the behaviors you are looking for? Look out for how candidates have phrased their answers: "I always ..." will be a general answer, and "I would" will be a hypothetical answer (which is fine when responding to a model answer-based question, but not in response to questions relating to their behaviors and strengths).

Stage 2—The Panel Discussion

When the panel members are ready the chairperson should ask each of them to state their ratings, which he or she should record on the overall panel rating form. Once the panel members have given their ratings the chairperson should reveal his or her own ratings. The reason for this is that the chairperson is usually the most senior member of the panel, and if he or she goes first, the other panel members may be influenced before fully discussing the ratings.

As with the sift, the panel should then discuss the ratings given for each criteria. Particular attention should be given to areas where panel members disagree. In these instances the chairperson should lead a structured discussion on the evidence considered by each panel member which led to their decision. The aim of the discussion should be to reach an agreed rating as a panel. When doing this remember that the person in the minority may be the one with the right rating—they may have identified evidence that their two colleagues have missed.

Stage 3—Agreeing and Recording the Ratings

As each of the criteria is discussed the chairperson should summarize the discussion, then check the proposed panel rating with the other members. Once it has been agreed it should be recorded by the chairperson on the panel rating form and discussion should move on to the next criteria.

Once ratings have been agreed for each of the criteria they should be added up to give the candidate's overall rating. The chairperson should complete the panel rating form with the panel's agreed comments and reasons for the overall rating. These comments should be brief and to the point, and must be directly related to the selection criteria. Remember that at some point in the future they may be seen by the candidate—as part of the feedback process, or in the event of an appeal against the panel's decision.

Selecting the Right Candidate

If the selection decision is based solely on the interview, and if you have followed the structured processes set out in this book, then this stage should be simple! At the end of the interviews you produce a ranking list (see example below), from the highest scoring candidate down to the lowest scoring candidate, and offer the job to the person at the top of the list.

The selection process is slightly more complicated if you have used some of the other assessment methods, set out in Chapter 9 of this book. You will need to consider their scores across the range of activities. You may have decided on a weighting system, for example:

- 50 percent of the final overall score based on performance at interview.

- 30 percent of the final overall score based on performance in assessment center activities.
- 20 percent of the final score based on performance in written tests.

However, there are circumstances when this is more complicated than it may first appear. If the process has gone well, you may end up with more than one candidate with an equally high score. If the process has gone badly, you may find that none of the candidates have reached the required level and that candidates who looked promising at the sift stage did not fulfill this promise at interview.

If you have two or more candidates with equal scores at the top of your list, you will need to re-examine the evidence they have presented. They may both have received the highest rating for a particular aspect of the assessment criteria, but is there anything in the evidence they presented which makes it possible to distinguish between them? For example:

- Both may have demonstrated extensive relevant knowledge and experience, but when you scrutinize it in detail one of them may have more complete all-round experience, or more relevant sector experience, or have managed at a more senior level.
- Both may have demonstrated excellent people management skills, but one of them may have done so in particularly challenging circumstances, such as managing a substantial restructuring program.

It is by looking in detail at the candidate's evidence against the requirements of your specification which will enable you to choose between two candidates who are closely matched.

If you scrutinize the evidence available and remain unable to decide between equally highly rated candidates you may decide to invite the candidates to return for a further interview, or test them using some of the other assessment methods set out in Chapter 9.

The opposite situation is that in which no candidates meet the required standard to be offered the post. It is not uncommon for candidates to score less well at interview than they did at the sift—part of the purpose of having an interview is to weed out those candidates who may have looked good on paper, but whose evidence does not stand up to being scrutinized through probing questioning.

In these circumstances it is sometimes tempting still to appoint the highest scoring candidate—after all, it avoids the expense and delay of going through the process of advertising, sifting, and interviewing all over again. Before doing this you should think carefully through the implications of taking on a candidate who may not be up to the job. It is not in anyone's interests for someone to be offered a post that is beyond them—it will be demoralizing for them, time consuming for you, disruptive to your team, and damaging to your organization's performance. It is better to examine why your recruitment process has not produced the right candidate, learn the necessary lessons then re-advertise the vacancy.

If you are applying the rating scale used throughout this book you should ensure that a candidate has scored a minimum of 2—*Applicant has provided sufficient evidence of the criteria to meet the required standard*—for each criteria before offering them the post. Table 8.1 shows an example of an interview rating list. A template for your own use can be found at Appendix 10.

Table 8.1 Interview rating list

	Candidate name	Score
1		
2		
3		
4		
5		

Signed...
Chair:
Member A:
Member B:
Date:

Summary of Chapter 8—After the Interview

In this chapter I have discussed what needs to happen after the interview. This begins when the candidate leaves the room, with the structured decision-making process involving:

- Individual ratings
- The panel discussion
- Agreeing and finalizing the panel ratings

Once the selection process is complete, a ranking list is drawn up.

CHAPTER 9

Other Assessment Methods

There are a number of other means of assessing candidates which can be used alongside, or even instead of, the traditional face-to-face interview. This chapter explores the pros and cons of these methods, and how they can be used effectively in order to enable you to make better recruitment decisions.

The methods I will be discussing are:

- Video interviewing
- Individual exercises
- Group exercises
- Doing the job
- Tests

Video Interviewing

In recent years it has become increasingly common for interviews to be conducted remotely by video link. This reflects:

- Changing work patterns—employees may be geographically remote from the organization's main offices.
- Resource constraints—it is expensive and time consuming to bring people to a central location for a comparatively short interview.
- Environmental concerns—unnecessary car journeys and air travel are damaging to the environment, as well as costly.
- Technological advances—broadband and remote video technology is now sufficiently reliable and secure to be used.

There are several options for conducting a video interview:

VOIP Services

The simplest way to conduct a video interview is by using VOIP services, such as Skype. The advantage of these services is ease of access—they can be used by anyone with a smartphone, tablet, or computer. However, services such as Skype do not provide a secure platform, so any sensitive information discussed in the interview may be at risk. Some businesses also feel that using such services to conduct interviews may not convey the right image for their organization.

Video Suites

Consultancy group KPMG decided not to use Skype, but have installed video suites at their offices so that candidates can attend for interview as close as possible to home. KPMG's director of People and Change, Kate Holt, feels that this approach strikes the right balance as "It retains the element of formality that interviews demand."

Recorded Interviews

Recorded interviews involve candidates receiving questions by e-mail, then videoing themselves answering the questions on a smartphone, tablet, or computer. They then upload their videos for recruiters to watch. These videos are usually quite short, no more than 10 minutes, so can be a quick way of sifting a large number of candidates. Their advantage over application forms is that they provide you with a fuller picture of the candidate, enabling you to see their demeanor and how they present themselves.

Limitations of Video Interviews

A video interview will provide you with a snapshot of a candidate, but not the level of detail that comes from a face-to-face meeting. Your view of a candidate's nonverbal communication will be incomplete, and may be distorted by something as simple as the positioning of the webcam. There is also the risk of being distracted from the content of the interview by technical issues, or by the environment surrounding the candidate.

Preparation is key to the effectiveness of video interviewing. Steps such as planning the interview and preparing your questions will be similar to face-to-face interviews, but in addition you will need to:

- Ensure that the technology is fit for purpose and working correctly.
- Ensure that panel members are familiar with how it works.
- Have immediate access to technical support if needed.
- Ensure that the interviewers' environment is appropriate for the interview.

While video interviews may form a useful part of the process, I recommend always conducting a face-to-face interview before making the final appointment.

Presentations

Asking candidates to deliver a presentation will be particularly relevant if the job requires the ability to communicate effectively with groups. Requiring candidates to deliver a presentation as part of the selection process will help you to assess their suitability for this part of the role.

If you are asking candidates to deliver a presentation you need to provide sufficient information for them to prepare. You may provide this in advance or on the day—the former will provide evidence of their ability to prepare thoroughly, whereas the latter will test their ability to work under pressure. In making your choice you will need to decide which will be more helpful to you in assessing their suitability for the job.

You will need to provide a clear briefing about the subject matter for the presentation. Normally this will be relevant to the job, which also means that the presentation can be used to help assess their subject knowledge. However, you may choose a subject that is less directly relevant—if you want to use the presentations to find out more about the candidates themselves, or simply to test their presentation skills in isolation from other factors.

You also have choices to make about the audience for the presentation. Options include:

- Presentation to the interview panel—this is easy to organize alongside the interview, and the presentation may provide the basis for some of your questions.
- Presentation to the interview panel and other candidates— this will enable you to see how the candidates' presentation skills compare, and also to see how they relate to each other, particularly if you build a question and answer activity into the presentations.
- Presentation to a wider group of your staff. This will enable you to consider a broader representation of views in selecting the successful candidate—for example, by getting the staff members in the audience to complete a brief observation sheet on each candidate's presentation.

Unless the ability to present is the main part of the job, for example, for a role such as a training officer, the presentation should not last too long. Ten minutes should be sufficient time for you to assess the candidate's skills. Candidates should be informed of how long they have and should be stopped as soon as their time runs out—this tests their time management skills, ensures that everyone is treated fairly, and enables you to keep to the timetable for the day.

The presentation may be followed by questions. This provides an opportunity for you to assess the candidates' ability to justify their points when challenged, or further explain their ideas.

Exercises

You may wish to set up individual or group exercises in order to observe and assess how candidates perform in relation to aspects of the performance criteria. Often a combination of exercises are used together to create an *assessment center*. Candidates' performance is observed and assessed to provide an all-round picture of their capabilities.

Individual Exercises

In-Tray

An in-tray exercise can be used to assess a candidate's ability to deal with the administrative and paper-based aspects of the job. The candidate is provided with an in-tray full of letters, reports, and messages and has to prioritize the tasks then carry them out. The exercise can be made more challenging by periodically adjusting instructions or adding material to the in-tray.

The in-tray exercise can be used to test criteria such as:

- Ability to prioritize
- Decision making
- Performance under pressure

Case Studies

Case studies can be written to reflect the types of situations that arise in carrying out the job. Candidates are required to identify not only what they would do, but also the decision-making process behind it, including their ability to identify and weigh up alternative courses of action before reaching their decision.

Reporting back on case studies may either be done verbally or in writing. The advantages of a verbal report back are that it provides further evidence of the candidate's presentation skills and an immediate opportunity to ask questions about their findings. The advantages of a written report are that it may go into greater depth, and provide evidence of the candidate's written skills. Once again, making the right choice will enable you to gather the evidence you need.

Individual Role Play

Role play exercises involve observing the candidate responding to and dealing with situations that may arise in the workplace. Care should be taken to ensure that the role play scenario is as realistic as possible. Candidates should be provided with sufficient briefing to be adequately prepared, but not so much that they are overloaded with information. The other part in the role play may be played by a member of the panel or another member of staff, but added realism and consistency can be achieved by employing an actor for the role.

Scenarios for role play may include:

- Responding to a dissatisfied customer.
- Negotiating with an assertive senior manager.
- Handling a disciplinary situation with a member of the team.

The role play will enable you to observe the candidate's interpersonal, communication, and decision-making skills. As with presentations, the role play can then provide the basis for the panel to ask questions arising which are relevant to the selection criteria.

Group Exercises

Group Role Play

Role play can also be used as a group activity. For example, each candidate might be assigned the part of a manager of a department in the organization, and have to make their case for extra funds to be allocated to their budget. This will test financial awareness, ability to make a persuasive case, and their skills in negotiating with the other candidates.

In this example you may bring in your finance director to make the decision about how the money should be allocated so that you, and your fellow panel members, can concentrate on observing how the candidates behave and interact in the group. Ideally each candidate should be monitored by a separate assessor—which makes it a resource-intensive activity.

As with the individual role play, care needs to be taken to provide the appropriate degree of briefing to the candidates. You also need to be careful when observing and assessing a group role play. There will inevitably be winners and losers at the end of the process, but it would be wrong to assume that the candidate who makes the best case for the extra funds is the candidate who has "won" the exercise. *How* people persuade and negotiate is as important as the outcome they achieve, and you should be looking for candidates who behave in accordance with the values of your organization.

Discussion Group

The discussion group involves candidates discussing or debating a topic. This may be general, such as "What do we mean by an ethical business?", or specific, such as "Identify five key steps that we could take to gain competitive advantage over our competitors."

The discussion group is observed in the same way as the group role play. It is a useful exercise for identifying candidates who demonstrate leadership skills, and also for identifying other roles that candidates take within the group. In this way you could link the exercise to psychometric tests, such as Belbin's Team Roles.

Practical Exercise

Practical exercises involve setting the group a specific task or challenge to achieve. The outdoors provides an opportunity for creating a more challenging environment, and there are plenty of centers that specialize in providing facilities for team activities. A typical outdoor exercise might involve supplying the group with the equipment needed to build a bridge across a stream or river.

Indoor activities tend to be less challenging, but are less expensive and time consuming to set up. There are numerous team activities that involve building structures with materials such as cardboard, drinking straws, and uncooked spaghetti!

The point of the activity is to assess the candidates' demonstration of competencies such as leadership, planning, and communication skills. As with the other team activities they will require close observation, ideally with one observer per candidate.

Doing the Job

Getting someone to do the job they have applied for can be one of the best ways of finding out how the candidate performs in the workplace.

Actors have to audition, and teachers have to demonstrate their ability to deliver a lesson. A well-known chain of sandwich shops has people work in its stores for a morning as part of the selection process. If the existing employees are not impressed, the candidate does not get through to the next stage!

Tests

There are numerous tests available that can be used as part of the selection process. Broadly speaking there are four main types, as shown in the Table 9.1 below.

Table 9.1 Four types of test

Type of Test	What it indicates	What it doesn't indicate
Skill/Aptitude	Nature and degree of capability or skill; degree of potential	Motivation Commitment
Personality	Presence of personality traits* which can then be related to those required for effective performance in the job	Knowledge Job performance
Psychometric	Combination of personality charac- teristics, values, and behavior, which can be related to those required for effective performance in the job	Knowledge Job performance
IQ	Intelligence	Personality traits Behavior Motivation Commitment Job performance

*Many personality tests are based on the "big five" traits—Openness, Conscientiousness, Extraversion, Agreeableness, and Neuroticism.

There are mixed views on the effectiveness of tests. Some advocates suggest that by using well-designed and reputable tests employers can increase their chances of selecting a candidate who will cope well with the job by up to 25 percent. However, a study in 1990 by Blinkhorn and Johnson concluded:

> ... we see little evidence that even the best personality tests predict job performance, and a good deal of evidence of poorly under-

stood statistical methods being pressed into service to buttress shaky claims.

What is clear is that it is essential to pay attention to selecting the right test for the role and your organization. For a post with high intellectual demands and limited social contact an IQ test may be most relevant. For managerial positions requiring the characteristics associated with Emotional Intelligence, a personality or psychometric test is more likely to provide the information you need.

You should also pay attention to who will interpret the results of the tests and how the results will be used. Many well-established personality tests were originally designed for use by psychologists, and risk being misinterpreted if the people analyzing the results have not had the appropriate training.

If tests are to be used it is worth investing not just in the instruments themselves, but in training your staff or utilizing external sources to ensure that they are interpreted correctly. This has become easier with the advent of the Internet, which makes it possible for results to be analyzed quickly and independently online.

Summary of Chapter 9—Other Assessment Methods

In this chapter I have discussed the following methods that can be used to assess candidates alongside the interview:

- Video interviewing
- Individual exercises
- Group exercises
- Doing the job
- Tests

We have discussed the pros and cons of each of these methods, and how to apply them effectively.

CHAPTER 10

Concluding the Recruitment Process

This chapter covers contacting the successful candidate, notifying unsuccessful candidates, taking up references, record keeping, and appointing the successful candidate.

Notifying the Successful Candidate

The chairperson may contact the highest scoring candidate and make them a verbal offer of employment, subject to references, once:

- The panel have agreed the ratings for all candidates and signed the ranking list.
- The candidate's entitlement to work in the country has been confirmed.
- The candidate's educational certificates and other documents have been seen and verified.

This should be done as soon as possible. A good candidate may be in demand, and the last thing you want is to offer them a job only to find they have been snapped up by one of your competitors!

If the candidate indicates that he or she wishes to accept the offer it should be confirmed in writing. If the candidate does not accept the offer, for example because they have just accepted the offer of another post, then you should ask them to confirm in writing that they are no longer interested in the post. This should be done as quickly as possible—an e-mail will be sufficient. Once you have received this you can then go on to offer the post to the second candidate on your list (assuming they have achieved the required score, of course!).

The verbal offer is also an opportunity to discuss the start date with the prospective employee.

The verbal offer should be followed up in writing using a letter that includes the following:

- Start date for employment
- Location
- Details of salary
- Details of working hours
- Period and nature of employment (i.e., permanent or fixed term)
- Details of probation period
- Other key benefits—for example, holiday entitlement
- Any other key conditions of employment

The letter should also make it clear if the employment offer is subject to conditions such as:

- Satisfactory references being obtained.
- Proof of the right to live and work in the United States being provided.
- Passing a Criminal Records check.
- Proof of qualifications.

Offer letters should be used in conjunction with full employment contracts—these may either be enclosed with the letter or sent out later by the HR Department.

Taking Up References

When you make the verbal offer to the successful candidate you should confirm that they have no objection to you taking up their references. This is not only a matter of courtesy, but it also helps establish the openness and trust which will provide a good foundation for the employer–employee relationship.

References should be used as means of confirming the information you have gained about the candidate from their application, interview, and other selection processes. They *should not* be requested as a means for distinguishing between two apparently equal candidates—this should be done by using the methods we have already discussed.

The main reason for this is that you should not place too much reliance on references, partly because the information they contain is notoriously unreliable! This is due to the following reasons:

- Employers fear legal action if they provide a bad reference.
- An employer may be keen to get rid of your candidate—their chances of doing so may be reduced if they provide you with an honest and detailed reference.
- Personal referees have been selected by the candidate—they are unlikely to be critical!
- References are often completed quickly and lack detail.

While the usefulness of obtaining references is limited, they provide the following benefits:

- Employer references are another means of confirming the candidate's identity.
- Employer references provide hard information, such as how long a person was in post, their job title, and their attendance record.
- Hopefully—confirmation of the information you have gained about the candidate and their abilities through the selection process.

If you find a reference bland or ambiguous you may wish to call the referee to obtain more detailed first-hand information about the candidate. If you decide to do this make sure you write down your questions in advance, so you can gain the required information in one call.

Notifying Unsuccessful Candidates

We have already noted that applicants who were unsuccessful at the sift stage are likely to be disappointed. This will be even more the case with candidates who are unsuccessful at interview. They have demonstrated a desire to work in your organization and probably put a good deal of time and effort into their application and interview. It is therefore important to be sensitive in the wording of the letter, in order to leave them with a positive impression of your organization and a feeling of having been treated respectfully and fairly.

You may have two categories of unsuccessful candidates:

1. Those who have not met the required standard to be appointed.
2. Those who met the required standard but were not at the top of your merit list.

Your letters should reflect this. Applicants from the second group should be told that they met the required standard, and that their papers will be kept on file in case a similar vacancy arises within the next six months.

You may wish to include some brief feedback in your letter, but should also offer the opportunity to receive verbal feedback from a member of the selection panel. You need to include:

- Which panel member should be contacted for feedback.
- When they can be contacted.
- How they can be contacted.

Feedback will normally be provided by phone or e-mail. If you are the panel member responsible for doing this ensure that you have the relevant papers to hand. When providing feedback you will need to strike the right balance between being positive and encouraging, for example, by recognizing areas where the applicant did well, while being very clear about where there were gaps between the evidence they presented and the required standard.

Remember that the purpose of feedback is to provide information which will be helpful to the recipient, and to do it in a way which will boost their confidence and self-esteem. Applying the BOOST acronym when providing feedback will help you to achieve this; remember that feedback should be:

Balanced—reflecting where the candidate did well, not just the areas where they need to be improved.
Objective—based on the evidence presented by the candidate.
Observed—based on your observations of the candidate during the recruitment process.

Specific—drawing upon specific examples of what they said or did when providing evidence.

Timely—the feedback should be provided as soon as possible after the completion of the recruitment process.

Seeking Feedback from Candidates

Feedback should be a two-way process, so as well as providing feedback to candidates you should seek feedback from them. You may ask them to complete a short questionnaire or online survey, including questions such as:

- Where did they see the vacancy advertised?
- Were they provided with the information they needed to know about the job and your organization?
- Was this information clearly written and presented?
- How could this information be improved?
- Were they satisfied with the way the process was conducted?
- Were there any aspects of the process which they felt could be improved?
- What is their impression of your organization?
- Would they be likely to apply for future jobs with your organization?
- What are their reasons for this?

The answers to these questions will help you plan future recruitment campaigns, and also provide you with valuable information about the candidates' perceptions of your organization.

Completing the Process

The recruitment process is almost at an end! Completing the process may include the following steps:

Record Keeping

Ensure that you have collected together the following documents:

- Candidates' application forms

- Interview notes
- Panel members' individual rating forms
- Panel rating forms
- Ranking list

These documents must be stored securely, either by the chair of the panel or by the HR Department. Electronic copies must be stored on a secure, password protected system, whereas paper documents should be retained in a locked cabinet in a secure environment. You may need to check your own organization's procedures and record keeping requirements.

Follow-Up Action

Actions will include:

- Initial contact with the successful candidate.
- Letter offering employment to the successful candidate.
- Reference requests.
- Ensuring relevant documentation has been checked—confirmation of right to work in the United States, educational certificates, and so on.
- Letters to unsuccessful candidates.

Reviewing the Recruitment Process

There is no such thing as a perfect recruitment process! The process should be evaluated in order to identify what went well, so that these points can be replicated in future, and what did not go well, so that these points can be addressed before the next recruitment exercise. Points to evaluate include:

- Did the job description and person specification accurately reflect the requirements of the job?
- Did the advertisement attract a diverse range of candidates of sufficient quality?
- Were the processes for managing applications and other documents efficient and effective?

- Did the interviews and other assessment activities run smoothly?
- If technology was used, was it fit for purpose?
- What feedback did you receive from candidates?
- Was the process successful in identifying a suitable candidate for the job?
- Are there any other lessons we can learn for future recruitment campaigns?

As well as reviewing the overall process, it is important to remember that every interview is an opportunity to learn and improve, so at the end of the day's interviewing the chairperson should lead a brief feedback discussion with the panel members. Each member of the panel should be invited to self-appraise their own performance, as well as providing feedback to each other. All panel members will bring different perspectives to this:

- The chairperson, as the senior member of the panel, will be able to draw upon greater experience.
- Specialist panel members, such as HR representatives or technical experts, will be able to offer independent insights.
- New panel members—while they may be less experienced— are also likely to have been more recently trained and may be able to (diplomatically) point out any bad habits!

Sitting on an interview panel can be a challenging experience and the chairperson should seek opportunities to provide constructive and encouraging feedback to less experienced colleagues.

Summary of Chapter 10—Concluding the Recruitment Process

The successful candidate should be contacted first verbally, then in writing. References should be taken up and any necessary checks should be made. The initial offer of employment will be subject to satisfactory completion of these.

Unsuccessful candidates should then be notified in writing and offered the opportunity to receive feedback. Feedback should meet the requirements of the BOOST acronym—Balanced, Objective, Observed, Specific, and Timely.

There should be a review of the recruitment process, identifying what went well and what needs to be improved for the next recruitment campaign. The review should include the opportunity for panel members to give feedback to each other.

The process should be completed by ensuring that all required paperwork has been completed and that records are complete and stored securely.

CHAPTER 11

Successful Induction

This chapter covers the benefits of effective induction, what to include in the induction process, what to avoid in the induction process, group induction, and evaluation of induction.

Once an appointment has been made it is tempting to think that the recruitment process is finished. However, if the aim is to ensure that recruitment is successful, it is important to pay attention to what happens next. All too often talented recruits leave their new organizations after only a few weeks in post, meaning that all the time and money spent on the recruitment process has been wasted. Often this is due to insufficient thought being given as to what will happen once the appointment has been made.

Effective Induction: The Benefits

Effective induction enables the new recruit to understand your organization, and how their role fits into the bigger picture. It provides them with an opportunity to meet and start building relationships with key people, and to develop their understanding of both the formal and informal cultures of the organization. Most importantly, it makes them feel welcomed.

Table 11.1 sets out the benefits of effective induction for both the employer and the new employee:

Table 11.1 Benefits of effective induction

Benefits to the employer	Benefits to the employee
Better return on investment in recruitment Better staff retention New employee becomes effective more quickly	Positive first experience of the organization Made to feel welcome Get to know key people and start building relationships
Boosts the morale of existing employees No need to repeat the recruitment process Enhances the reputation of your organization	Clarity as to what the job involves Become productive more quickly More likely to fulfill their potential as an employee

Pay and Remuneration

One of the worst things an organization can do with a new employee is fail to pay them on time. This is surprisingly common, particularly in bureaucratic organizations with complex and time-consuming processes for getting things done.

The result of a delay in pay will certainly damage the new employee's perception of the organization. It may also present them with practical difficulties, affecting their ability to meet their financial commitments. And dealing with a delay in pay will certainly divert their attention from what you want them to be focusing on, which is learning about their new job.

For these reasons, it is important that issues relating to pay are quickly addressed on appointment.

Formal and Informal Organizational Culture

Induction processes are often very clear about the formal aspects of the organization—the espoused vision, values, and corporate objectives, and ways of working to achieve these. However, it is equally important to pay attention to the informal aspects of organizational culture. What conversations go on around the water cooler? Are the things that people say informally supportive of your organization's vision, values, and strategy, or do people look for opportunities to overtly or covertly undermine them?

If it is the latter, you need to be careful that the new employee is not unduly influenced by these undermining voices. There may be wider issues about the culture of the organization that you need to address—indeed, you may have recruited with a view to bringing in people who will change the culture of the organization. If there are negative voices at work in your organization you will need to be prepared to address these, by tackling the views they are presenting of your organization while also ensuring that you present a positive view to the new recruit.

What to Include in the Induction Process?

Points to include in induction will vary according to the requirements of the role and the nature of the organization. The list below outlines some of the key areas to consider including in your induction process.

Pre-Employment

- Joining instructions.
- Proof of the legal right to work in the country (if required, and not already done during recruitment).
- New starter forms (enabling the setup of bank account details and eligible benefits from day one).
- Employment contract (to be signed before the employee takes up the post).*
- Conditions of employment (to be read and signed before the employee takes up the post).*
- Company literature and website/social media.

*Two copies of the contract and conditions of employment should be provided and signed; one to be retained by the employer, and the other to be retained by the employee.

Health and Safety, and Compliance

- Emergency exits
- Evacuation procedures
- First aid facilities
- Health and safety policy
- Accident reporting
- Protective clothing
- Specific hazards
- Security procedures
- Confidentiality
- Data protection

Much of this information will be set out in documents such as office risk assessments, local instructions on managing incidents, and company policies and procedures. New employees should be provided with these, but not just left to read them. Little information will be absorbed, and you will be left with a bored and unmotivated employee! It is important for you and experienced colleagues to talk the new employee through relevant procedures, and to explain why they are important. Tests and validation exercises are a useful way of checking understanding. I know of one organization which required new recruits to complete a corporate jigsaw, acquiring pieces as they met new people until the jigsaw was complete.

Facilities

- Site map.
- Refreshments—kitchen, staff restaurant, vending machines, and so on.
- Information about local facilities—shops, cafes, restaurants, banks, and so on.
- First aid post (and details of who is qualified to administer first aid).
- Guided tour of the building and explanation of local procedures.
- Telephone and computer system information.
- Security pass.
- Car park pass.
- Opening hours.
- Remote/flexible working tools and access to work systems, if applicable.

Organizational Information

- Organization background and history
- Organization chart—national/global
- Organization chart—departmental
- Organization strategy
- Products and services
- Quality systems and processes
- Customer care policy

Culture and Values

- Mission statement
- Corporate vision
- Employer brand
- Values

Benefits and Policies

- Pay—payment date and method.
- Tax and national insurance.
- Workplace/stakeholder pension schemes.
- Other benefits.
- Expenses and expense claims.
- Working time, including hours, flexitime, and arrangements for breaks.
- Remote working policies.
- Holidays, special leave.
- Probation period.
- Equality and diversity policies.
- Well-being strategy, including attendance/absence policy and procedures.
- Internet, intranet, e-mail, and social media policies.
- Performance management system.
- Discipline procedure.
- Grievance procedure.
- Employee groups.

Role-Specific Information

- Clear outline of the job/role requirements.
- Introduction to colleagues.
- Ways of working.
- Meeting with key colleagues (either face-to-face, or through the use of technology).
- Organizational orientation; demonstration of how the employee fits into the team and how their role fits with the overall strategy and goals.

Learning and Development

- Continuing professional development—expectations and opportunities.
- In-house development opportunities.
- External opportunities.
- Career development.

What to Avoid in the Induction Process

There is a delicate balance to be struck between providing the new recruit with clear and comprehensive information relating to their new role, and overloading them with so much detail that it's impossible for them to take it all in. Be careful to guard against the following pitfalls:

- Providing too much, too soon—the inductee must not be overwhelmed by a mass of information on the first day. Keep it simple and relevant.
- Pitching presentations at an inappropriate level—where possible, presentations should be tailored to take into account prior knowledge. Having conversations to establish what a new employee already knows is a great way of building your relationship with them, and of validating their existing knowledge. It will also provide you with the opportunity to address any misconceptions they may have formed about their new role and organization.
- Too much information being provided centrally, often by the HR Department, rather than local managers. Induction should be a shared process, with centrally generated information being supported by local input.
- Creating an induction program that generates unreasonable expectations by overselling the job. By all means talk to the new recruit about career opportunities in your business, but be realistic about the requirements of the existing job and the need to fully demonstrate these before further developing their career.
- Creating an induction program that focuses only on administration and compliance and does not reflect organizational

values. This can make induction feel like a very mechanical process which is dull and uninspiring for the new employee. An effective induction program should be engaging and assure the new employee that they have made the right decision to join the business.

Group Induction

If a significant number of new recruits join at the same time it might be appropriate to run a group induction exercise. This enables resources to be used efficiently, avoids duplicating the same presentations and conversations over and over again, and ensures that consistent messages are provided to new recruits.

The advantages of group induction are:

- It saves inductors' and managers' time by dealing with a group rather than several individuals. The use of digital tools to share information can be useful where new recruits are globally dispersed.
- It ensures that all new recruits are given a consistent positive message portraying a clear employer brand, values, and culture.
- A range of engaging communication techniques can be deployed, such as group discussions or projects.
- It enables new recruits to socialize with each other and build cross-functional relationships.

However, there are also disadvantages which include:

- It may contain a range of subjects that are unlikely to appeal to a cross-functional and mixed ability group of new employees.
- It may take place several weeks, or even months, after the inductee joins the organization, which disrupts integration into the work team and risks information being shared too late in the induction process.
- It can be less personal, and involve managers and HR personnel rather than colleagues and local supervisors.

As with the recruitment process, a blended approach is often most effective, enabling new recruits to hear centrally generated messages alongside learning about their new job and organization from their line manager and immediate colleagues.

Evaluating the Induction Process

The induction process should be monitored to determine whether it is meeting the needs of the new recruits and the organization. Monitoring should include opportunities for feedback at the end of the induction process, and encouraging new recruits to highlight areas for improvement.

As well as gathering feedback from new employees, it is important to identify in advance your measures of success of the induction process and to evaluate the process against these. Information from turnover statistics and exit interviews can also be used. It will be particularly relevant to look at those from employees who leave within the first 12 months. This information will help you to refine your recruitment and induction processes, as well as enabling you to identify and address any themes which emerge about underlying issues in your organization.

Summary of Chapter 11—Successful Induction

In this chapter I have set out the importance of effective induction in ensuring that there is a return on the investment made in the recruitment process. I have identified what should be included in the induction process, which should be a combination of hard information about policies and procedures relating to the role, an insight into the culture and priorities of the organization, and local information relating to the new employee's immediate team and workplace.

Induction should provide the opportunity for the new recruit to build relationships with their line manager, immediate colleagues, other new recruits, and key people throughout the organization. Above all, induction should be a process of welcoming the new recruit into the organization.

CHAPTER 12

International Recruitment

This chapter covers key issues to consider in international recruitment, including the cultural environment, cultural differences, and methods of recruitment and selection.

Much of the good practice set out in this book will apply equally to recruitment in the international environment. However, there are additional challenges to be addressed when recruiting internationally. Recruiters need to be mindful of cultural differences, and their impact on the recruitment process. There may also be different legislative requirements relating to recruitment. Responding to these factors effectively will reinforce your organization's reputation as an ethical business. Get it wrong, and your reputation will be damaged.

Key Questions to Consider

Before launching a recruitment campaign, there are some key questions to consider:

- Where in the world is it most appropriate for employees to be located? In answering this question issues such as the cost of labor, relevant experience, infrastructure, quality of service, and impact on employment relationships in the home country, all need to be addressed.
- Where in the world is there increasing demand for goods and services? An organization might identify a new market that it wants to move into. Is this achieved most appropriately by providing the service or goods from existing locations, or is there a need to move into a new location?
- Is it most appropriate to employ local people, or to move existing employees from other countries to a new location?

Employing local people will usually be cheaper (because of the costs associated with employing expatriates) and will mean that they have local knowledge. However, it might be necessary to move some existing employees, so that their knowledge and experience of the organization can be used.

- What are the costs associated with employment in different countries? Costs of recruitment itself need to be considered, as well as the costs of shedding staff (which can be very expensive in many European countries).
- What are the restrictions placed by legislation? This could be legislation relating to immigration, or could it be local labor laws that need to be complied with in the recruitment process.

The Cultural Environment

You will also need to consider the cultural environment in which you are recruiting. National cultures tend to be reflected in corporate cultures, and these vary widely around the world. With this in mind, Fons Trompenaars has identified four different types of corporate culture:

1. *The Family culture*—hierarchical but people-oriented, with relationships playing a key role. Senior figures are respected, younger ones indulged. Characteristic of Japanese and Italian organizations.
2. *The Eiffel Tower*—hierarchical, narrow at the top and broad at the base. The structure is rigid with clear division of labor, clearly defined roles and functions. The rigid bureaucracy makes change complex and time consuming. Characteristic of French and German organizations.
3. *The Guided Missile*—egalitarian, not hierarchical. Driven by tasks, not people. The guided missile culture values the end result above everything else. Characteristic of companies in the United States and United Kingdom.
4. *The Incubator*—where individual development is more important than the organization itself. People are liberated from routines and encouraged to be innovative. Start-up companies in Silicon Valley are examples of incubator cultures.

This raises some interesting questions regarding recruitment. Employees will need different sets of skills, attributes, and attitudes to be successful in each of the different corporate cultures. So if your organization is a "guided missile" company, moving into a country with a tradition of "family" or "Eiffel Tower" corporate cultures, which set of skills, attributes, and attitudes are you looking for? A fundamental decision needs to be made as to whether you will look to recruit people who best match your organization's corporate culture, or adapt your culture to the local business environment.

There is no clear answer to this, and examples can be found of organizations which have adopted both approaches. There are those who take pride in working in the same way, wherever they are in the world. Japanese manufacturing companies expect their employees to apply the principles of "Kaizen," no matter where their factories may be located. However, there are also many international companies with local subsidiaries which would be unrecognizable as the same company, save for their logo and branding. The corporate objectives may be the same, but the way they go about achieving them are fundamentally different.

Cultural Differences

When recruiting in a cross-cultural environment you will need sufficient cultural awareness to ensure that you conduct the process fairly. It is also important to remember that different organizations and industries tend to develop their own cultures, not just different nations. Some points to consider include:

- *Communication styles*
Some cultures, such as the United States, tend to value direct styles of communication, whereas others, such as Japan and India, place more emphasis on building relationships before getting down to business. This may present challenges in a recruitment interview, where only a limited amount of time is available for candidates to demonstrate their suitability for the job. Interviewers need to strike the right balance. On the one hand, we have established the importance of taking time to build rapport at the start of the interview. On the other hand, interviewers need to

be prepared to ask direct questions and use techniques such as assertive interruptions to keep discussion on track once the interview is under way.

- *Degrees of formality*

An interview is a formal process, but the degree of formality with which it is conducted will vary across cultures. Organizational culture is as important as national culture—a creative start-up is likely to adopt a more informal approach to interviewing candidates, perhaps over a coffee or via a video link. In this culture less formal styles of dress are likely to be seen as appropriate—a male candidate is unlikely to be expected to wear a collar and tie, for example.

A more conservative organization, such as a government service, is more likely to interview candidates across a desk, and more likely to expect candidates to be formally dressed.

As panel members, you need to be very clear about the criteria against which you are assessing the candidate. If "smart appearance" is specified in the criteria you may take it into account in your assessment, but if not, you must stick to assessing the candidate against the stated criteria.

- *Shaking hands*

In most countries business people greet each other with a handshake. In some countries this is not appropriate between genders.

There is also the risk that some panel members may view a soft hand-shake as a sign of weakness, whereas others perceive a firm handshake as aggressive. It is unlikely that the quality of the handshake was part of your stated assessment criteria! So panel members must go back to the principle of "notice the first thought, act on the second"; be aware of your reaction to the handshake, but remind yourself that this is not relevant to the criteria against which you are assessing the candidate.

As set out in Chapter 5, you should agree your approach to shaking hands before the interviews start. If in doubt, don't! But equally if a candidate offers their hand you should respond—don't leave them standing there feeling embarrassed.

- *Eye contact*

In western cultures strong, direct eye contact conveys confidence and sincerity. In South America it is seen as a sign of trustworthiness. However, in some cultures, such as Japan, prolonged eye contact is considered rude and is generally avoided.

As an interviewer you should make the degree of eye contact which feels appropriate to you. Be responsive to the candidate—if they look uncomfortable with the level of eye contact then reduce it. Most importantly, remember that you are assessing candidates on the basis of the evidence they present, not whether they look you in the eye while doing so.

- *Responses to questions*

In some cultures, for example, Korea, it is a mark of respect to remain silent when asked a "good question." However, in cultures such as the United States and the United Kingdom, to remain silent when asked a question may be seen as rude, or as evidence of the candidate's inability to provide an answer. In this situation you may need to "give permission" for the candidate to respond, by gently prompting and encouraging them.

- *Gift giving*

In some cultures gift giving is an accepted part of business protocol. In the United States, this may be viewed with suspicion or even as corruption. For this reason, any gift offered by a candidate to a member of an interview panel should be politely but firmly refused.

The best way to respond to these cultural differences, and to ensure that they do not affect the outcome of the process for the candidate, is to remember that the purpose of the interview is to assess the candidate's competence. Your assessment should solely relate to the evidence they present. If you feel that any of your fellow panel members are straying from this principle you should raise it with them in the panel discussion.

Methods of Recruitment

There are four methods that are likely to be particularly relevant to international recruitment.

Headhunting

There are a number of specialist organizations which operate international search and selection. They can provide specific knowledge and expertise which you may not have within your organization. However, their fees are also likely to be expensive, making it an approach to recruitment that is only appropriate for the most senior or specialist roles.

Cross-National Advertising

As with all resourcing, advertising remains a common way of attracting people to relevant jobs. There are considerable differences in the use of advertising. The trends vary across sectors, but there has been a general shift away from newspapers and journals to more creative or online approaches. In some societies, such as India, access to the Internet remains limited, meaning that other creative approaches may be required. One example is the use of targeted outdoor posters in locations such as railway stations and other key commuter routes, which help to ensure that advertising reaches its target audience.

It is also worth bearing in mind that, in many parts of the world, national borders are no longer seen as a constraint as to where people are willing to work. In the European Union, for example, someone living in Luxemburg could easily travel to work in Germany, France, or Belgium. This should be taken into account when deciding where advertisements should be placed.

Online Recruitment

Searching the Internet has become the dominant approach for individuals seeking roles, particularly senior professionals, technical specialists, and managers. The advantages for recruiting organizations include volume and geographic spread of applicants, 24 hours a day access to vacancies, and an opportunity to promote the brand of the organization through its online presence. However, there may also be challenges caused by reliability of the technology, and ensuring that your vacancy stands out in a crowded marketplace.

International Graduate Programs

Graduates provide a source of talent for international roles as they often see such openings as being key to their career development. They may also be more mobile than other more established employees as they are less likely to have the same family ties. However, there are more factors to take into account than a simple readiness to be internationally mobile.

Organizations might be tempted to question the return on investment as graduate retention is not always high. In some cultures age or experience is associated with status, making it difficult for young graduates to succeed in leadership and management roles.

Selection Methods

There are differences in the use and acceptance of different selection methods in different countries. For example, the use of graphology (analysis of an individual through samples of their handwriting) is relatively common in France and Switzerland, but is hardly used anywhere else in the world (possibly because there is little evidence to suggest that it is reliable). In the main, international recruitment relies on the methods we have already discussed, primarily interviews, assessment centers, and psychological tests. However, there are particular points to consider when applying these methods in the international environment.

Interviews

Interviews are commonly used, but the approach to them differs. In the United States and United Kingdom, it is common for interviews to follow the structured processes set out in this book, where candidates are systematically questioned against the same set of criteria. In other cultures interviews are conducted differently. They may be less structured, or based more on identifying whether the candidate is likely to be a "good fit" with the culture of the organization (e.g., would they accept their place within an Eiffel Tower hierarchy?). In other cultures knowledge and education are highly valued, so these areas may be the focus of questions at interview.

As already discussed, there are also cultural differences in the ways in which applicants will react in an interview situation. It is important to be sensitive to these, and not to give undue weight to responses you initially find surprising. Cultural awareness training may be helpful for panel members, and, when recruiting internationally, it might be helpful to have someone from the prevailing local culture as one of the panel members. Above all, remember that you are assessing candidates against the specified abilities required to do the job.

Assessment Centers

It is important to remember that assessment centers are still relatively unknown in many countries, so you may have to overcome the "shock of the new" if you decide to use this approach. You will need to clearly specify the activities involved, and give clear reasons as to why you are using them.

In designing assessment center activities it is important to ensure that they are free of cultural bias, and that the results are interpreted appropriately. It is also important that assumptions are not made about the exposure that applicants have had to technology. Applicants based in the United States or Europe are likely to feel reasonably comfortable if asked to carry out a computer-based assessment, but an applicant from a developing country might be put at a disadvantage simply due to a lack of familiarity with the technology.

Psychological Testing

Using psychological tests attracts some controversy, particularly when they are applied in international settings. If psychological tests are to be used the following points need to be considered:

- What norms are being used as a comparator? If the norms are based on sections of the population of the United States, are they appropriate when assessing people from another country? This is particularly relevant in relation to personality assessment tests.
- Do the questions have any cultural bias? For example, are words used that have one meaning in one country and another in a different country? Could this result in an applicant answering a question wrongly?
- Are the assessments available in the applicants' first language? If the applicant is required to translate questions this may have an effect on performance. If the test has been translated from another language, is the translation accurate and free from ambiguity?
- Are the tests discriminatory in any way?

While the insights from psychological assessments may still provide valuable insights for recruiters, these questions strongly suggest that they should be used with caution. Certainly they should be used alongside other methods, and undue weight should not be given to test answers in isolation from other sources of evidence.

Summary of Chapter 12—International Recruitment

In this chapter I have considered some of the specific issues that may arise in international recruitment. It is important to consider these issues in advance, and to develop your understanding of the cultural environment in which you are recruiting. This includes developing your understanding of cultural norms and differences, so you can ensure that the recruitment process is fair to all candidates and that they are all assessed fairly and equally against the specified criteria for the role. There are particular issues with the use of psychological assessments, which should be used and interpreted with caution.

Conclusion

The Future of Recruitment

This concluding chapter covers how technology and other emerging trends might affect the defining of role requirements, attracting the right candidates, sifting, interviewing, and other assessment methods.

This book reflects current best practice in recruitment, with a view to helping recruiters to succeed in appointing the best candidates for the job. However, this is in a context which is constantly, and rapidly, changing. Technological developments mean that we are able to use approaches in recruitment which were not possible a decade ago. Developments in behavioral science mean that we are increasingly aware of the impact of bias when making recruitment decisions, and of the need to reduce this in order to ensure that recruitment decisions are as rational and objective as possible. So it's an evolving picture.

I will conclude by considering emerging trends in recruitment, and how best practice may evolve over the next few years.

Defining Requirements for the Role

Traditionally requirements were defined by a job description, setting out the purpose and main tasks of the role. Candidates were then assessed on the basis of their experience in carrying out those tasks, and the candidate with the most relevant experience was appointed. Younger candidates would have the opportunity to be taken on as apprentices, and learn from their more experienced colleagues.

The problem with these approaches are that they are essentially backward looking, in a fast-changing world. Experience of doing things in a particular way over many years may not relate to how they will need to be done in the future. Nor do people with many years' experience necessarily bring the required attitudes to their work. They may become cynical, disillusioned, or just bored—not the people you want to be influencing your apprentices. They may also feel threatened by and be suspicious of new working methods and, in the worst instances, seek to undermine them.

So paying excessive regard to experience in the recruitment process has demonstrable risks. In response to these there has been a move away from recruiting on the basis of candidates' ability to meet the requirements of a job description, to an increased emphasis on person specifications. As already discussed, the person specification focuses on the qualities of the individual alongside the requirements of the job. Alongside experience it specifies qualifications required for the role, enabling recruiters to see whether a candidate has invested time in their continuing professional development, and keeping their qualifications up to date. It looks at whether they have the underpinning knowledge to be effective in the role, and again, what they have done to keep this up to date. Most crucially the person specification defines the competencies required to be effective in the role, and provides candidates with the opportunity to provide evidence of how they have demonstrated these.

However, there remains a concern that person specifications still essentially look backwards. This can be addressed to some extent by including competencies such as the ability to adapt to change, or to new working methods, and to test candidate's ability to respond effectively in these situations. But there remains a concern that candidates with less experience, but greater long-term potential, may still be missing out.

In order to address this some organizations are now going beyond the use of person specifications and developing "success profiles," which provide a fuller and more rounded picture of the attributes required for the role. The five elements of a success profile are:

- Strengths—the strengths required in a role; that a job holder would need to feel motivated by, do regularly and do well, in order to succeed in the role.
- Behaviors—the actions and activities that result in effective performance in the job.
- Ability—the aptitude or potential to perform to the required standard.

- Experience—the knowledge or mastery of an activity or subject gained through involvement in it over a period of time.
- Technical—the demonstration of specific professional skills and knowledge (may be evidenced through relevant professional qualifications).

When devising success profiles recruiters should look ahead and identify the attributes required to do the job effectively over the next three to five years, instead of looking backwards at how the job has been done in the past.

When drafting person specifications and success profiles, the importance of paying close attention to the language used is increasingly being recognized. The "tech speak" used to describe specialized roles may only be accessible to people who already have experience in that sector, once again meaning that you may fail to reach people with more long-term potential. In many sectors technical roles have historically been filled by men, leading to gender bias in the recruitment process, due to the tendency for people to recruit in their own image. Changing the language used when talking about these jobs is one way of starting to address the problem and appeal to a wider workforce. Software Company Atlassian reported an 80 percent increase in the global hiring of women after analyzing and changing the language used in its job advertisements.

Through taking this broader approach to defining role requirements, it should be possible to strike a better balance when making assessment decisions, taking into consideration potential alongside experience.

Attracting the Right Candidates

As reflected in Chapter 3, the days of drafting an advertisement and placing it in a newspaper or trade journal, then sitting back and waiting for applications to flood in, are long gone. The Internet, and particularly social media, are transforming the ways in which people look for opportunities, and recruiting organizations need to be responsive to this.

With figures suggesting that up to 49 percent of employed Americans are looking for new jobs on social networks, it is hardly surprising that 55 percent of companies plan to increase spending on utilizing social media for hiring. Where you make this investment depends on the nature of the applicants you are trying to attract. If you are looking for business professionals, then business-focused sites such as LinkedIn will enable you to attract the right applicants. An increasing number of companies are not only using LinkedIn to identify potential employees, but are also sifting and shortlisting on the basis of people's LinkedIn profiles.

If, on the other hand, you wish to reach a broader range of applicants, including people who may not currently be in work, then sites such as Facebook may provide the right vehicle. And if you wish to attract a younger workforce, then WhatsApp or Snapchat may be more helpful in reaching the right demographic.

Advertising vacancies should only be one part of your organization's social media presence. There should be a wider strategy of building the organization's social media profile, making people aware of your organization's vision, values, and achievements. If this is done well then you will become an organization that people actively want to work for, with potential candidates contacting you about opportunities before they even arise. These contacts should be recorded on a database, and invited to apply when it is time for you to recruit. Other applicants will see your advertisement and be able to make a quick decision about applying for a post with your organization, on the basis of what they already know about you from your social media profile.

So in the main, judicious use of social media is likely to be the key to attracting new talent and making people aware of opportunities when they arise. One exception to this may be in international recruitment where, in developing nations, access to the Internet remains less widespread than in more developed economies. If the applicants you are targeting do not have easy Internet access then you will need to find other ways of reaching them, as discussed in Chapter 12. However, the World Wide Web is, increasingly, as the name suggests, worldwide, and the future trend will be toward methods that utilize the Internet effectively.

Sifting

Technology is increasingly a feature of the sifting stage. It has the logistical benefits of streamlining processes and reducing the time demands made on recruiters, who usually have to find time for their involvement in recruitment alongside their other responsibilities.

It may be suggested that removing human input from the sifting stage can be seen as a benefit. As we have seen, humans risk falling foul of all sorts of forms of conscious and unconscious bias, whereas technology is seen as neutral. However, as reflected in Chapter 4, technology is not immune from bias. After all, it is programmed by humans! So there is a risk of technology perpetuating existing norms in the sector, and discriminating against high potential candidates who differ from these.

So at the moment the technology is flawed, but plenty of tech companies are working on developing artificial intelligence–enhanced selection tools with a view to addressing these risks. These include gamified psychometric tests, and the development of algorithms which are designed to balance diversity requirements with quantifiable data on individual performance.

Where human input continues to be involved in sifting, there are steps that can be taken to increase fairness and reduce the risk of bias. Research suggests that better recruitment decisions are made when three or more people are involved in making decisions, particularly if they are a diverse group from different roles and levels within the organization. If these individuals come to their initial decisions independently, and are encouraged to question and challenge each other's decisions, then the chances of reliable sift decisions are increased. In order for this to happen organizations need to create a culture where senior people are positive about the benefits of being challenged.

Use of approaches such as blind recruitment are likely to increase, where sifters do not have access to biographical information about applicants, meaning that decisions are made solely on the evidence of their abilities to do the job. However, technology has also enabled an opposing trend, where applicants are sifted on the basis of video evidence uploaded from their mobile phones. This may be helpful if you are looking for candidates who display particular behaviors or characteristics; for example, extrovert behaviors in the hospitality industries. This, of course, opens the doors to just the kind of instantaneous, and potentially biased, decision making, that approaches such as blind recruitment are designed to address. So the debate is likely to rumble on.

Interviewing

The trend in interviewing is toward the use of a blended approach, which is a particularly good fit with the use of success profiles in defining role requirements. The use of a blended interview, often alongside other assessment methods, enables a diverse range of criteria to be tested.

As discussed earlier in this book, structured interviews are proven to be more reliable in generating reliable evidence of a candidate's abilities than other types of interview. But in many instances they have become predictable and formulaic, enabling candidates to reel off well-rehearsed answers which provide panel members with what they want to hear. They do not test a candidate's ability to think on their feet, and respond to a question which they may not have anticipated; or test their ability to apply their skills effectively across a range of situations.

There is also some evidence that, in some quarters, the competency-based approach is considered outmoded. Some organizations have addressed this by simply rebranding their competencies as "behaviors," and ended up testing much the same things as before. It is more realistic to recognize the benefits of using a competency-based approach, while also recognizing that a strictly defined interviewing approach of constantly testing competency-based criteria with a repetitive range of behavioral questions can act as an unnecessary constraint on interviewers.

Blended interviews allow competencies (or behaviors) to be tested at interview alongside other criteria such as strengths, technical knowledge, and experience. "What would you do if?" questions can be used to test those candidates who have potential, but as yet lack the relevant experience. The outcome of such an approach is a broader picture of the candidate's abilities than that gained through a purely behavioral interview.

Aligned with increasingly diverse panels, as for the sifting stage, this approach should provide a process that is both fairer and more reliable than those used in the past.

Technology is also changing the way in which interviews are conducted. Swedish company Furhat Robotics has even developed a robot interviewer, named Tengai, which is able to ask questions to candidates and react to their answers. Tengai's creators claim that she is free of the biases and prejudices which afflict human interviewers although, as we have already discussed, that will depend on who is programming the robot in the first place. Her opening question:

Have you been interviewed by a robot before?

As video conferencing becomes increasingly reliable, candidates can be interviewed from anywhere in the world. This is likely to increase still further with the development of three-dimensional hologram projections. With these technological leaps remote interviewing will become increasingly common, reducing both the financial and environmental costs of unnecessary travel.

Other Assessment Methods

Alongside blended interviews, organizations are increasingly utilizing a range of assessment methods to get a fuller picture of candidates' abilities. We have seen some of the ways in which technology will change how candidates' abilities can be assessed. Gamification will make simulations increasingly realistic, and by building assessments into these programs we can again reduce the risk of assessor bias. Alternatively, it will also become increasingly easy to see how candidates cope in real-life situations, instead of having to use simulations. Candidates will be able to upload videos of themselves carrying out relevant activities, using technology such as smartwatches and platforms such as Snapchat.

Whether or not they use technology, corporations are increasingly going beyond the interview and using a variety of methods to assess their candidates. TGI Friday look for candidates who can generate the "Friday's feeling"—difficult to assess just through an interview. So their assessment process involves two days of interviews and a range of activities, with a view to testing candidates' creativity, ability to engage with customers, and ability to work effectively as a member of a team. The length of the process is as significant as its content, in differentiating between those candidates whose enthusiasm is short-lived, and those who are able to sustain it.

The approaches you use depend on the nature of your organization—not every business needs an all singing and dancing team of extroverts. But if you do, then you'd better test their ability to sing and dance. And if you don't—then you need to define clearly what you do need, and put in place the right combination of activities to test for it.

Appendices

Templates for Your Own Use

Appendix 1—Job Description

Appendix 2—Person Specification

Appendix 3—Application form

Appendix 4—Panel member rating form

Appendix 5—Panel rating form

Appendix 6—Interview timetable

Appendix 7—Interview plan

Appendix 8—Interview preparation sheet

Appendix 9—Interview record sheet

Appendix 10—Interview rating list

Appendix 1

Job Description

Job Title:

Grade:

Salary Band:

This post is based:

Reports to:
Budgetary Responsibility:

Staff Charge:

Job Purpose

Key Responsibilities

Appendix 2

Person Specification

Criteria	Essential	Desirable	How assessed
KNOWLEDGE			Application form Interview Tests
QUALIFICATIONS			Documents to be provided
EXPERIENCE			Application form Interview References
COMPETENCIES			Application form Interview References

Appendix 3

Application Form

Important Information for Applicants

The person specification sets out the criteria that are essential or desirable for this job. Where the method of assessment is stated to be the application form, your application needs to demonstrate clearly and concisely how you meet each of the criteria, even if other methods of assessment are also shown. If you do not address these criteria fully, or if we do not consider that you meet them, you will not be shortlisted. Please give specific examples wherever possible.

Equality and Diversity

We are committed to and champion equality and diversity in all aspects of our work. All employees are expected to understand and promote our equality and diversity policy in the course of their work.

---

1. Personal Details

Name	
Contact address	
Contact telephone number(s)	Daytime: Evening: Mobile:
E-mail address	

2. Experience

Give brief details of your experience and your achievements, beginning with your current or most recent post. You should demonstrate how your experience meets the following requirements:

Dates	Post held	Brief details of experience and achievements

3. Competencies

These are the skills and attributes required to perform the duties of this role effectively.
Provide specific examples of no more than 200 words to demonstrate how you meet the following criteria.

| |
| |
| |

<table>
<tr><td></td></tr>
<tr><td></td></tr>
<tr><td></td></tr>
</table>

4. Qualifications

5. Other Requirements

Copies will be required.

6. References

Please provide the name and contact details of two referees, at least one of whom should be able to comment directly on your performance at work.

Please note that referees will only be contacted if you demonstrate the required criteria at interview.

Referee 1	Referee 2
Name:	Name:
Address:	Address:
Job Title (if applicable):	Job Title (if applicable):
Daytime phone no.:	Daytime phone no.:
E-mail:	E-mail:

Thank you for applying for this post. We will contact you by e-mail by [INSERT DATE] *to let you know whether you are invited for interview.*

Appendix 4

Panel Member Rating Form

Name of Applicant:

Date:

Sift/Interview (Please delete as appropriate)

Please rate each criteria in accordance with the following rating scale:

Score	Definition
0	Applicant has not provided any relevant evidence of this criteria
1	Applicant has provided insufficient evidence of this criteria to meet the required standard
2	Applicant has provided sufficient evidence of this criteria to meet the required standard
3	Applicant has provided strong evidence of this criteria to exceed the required standard

Criteria	Score	Comments
Total		

Signed:

Name:

Date:

Appendix 5

Panel Rating Form

Name of Applicant:

Date:

Sift/Interview (Please delete as appropriate)

Please rate each criteria in accordance with the following rating scale:

Score	Definition
0	Applicant has not provided any relevant evidence of this criteria
1	Applicant has provided insufficient evidence of this criteria to meet the required standard
2	Applicant has provided sufficient evidence of this criteria to meet the required standard
3	Applicant has provided strong evidence of this criteria to exceed the required standard

Criteria	Chair	Member A	Member B	Panel's Agreed Rating
Total				

Comments and Reasons for the agreed rating:

Signed ...

Chair:

Member A

Member B:

Date:

Appendix 6

Interview Timetable

9.00	Panel convenes
9.15	Prepare Interview 1
9.30	Interview 1
10.15	Assess Candidate 1
10.30	Break
10.45	Prepare Interview 2
11.00	Interview 2
11.45	Assess Candidate 2
12.00	Prepare Interview 3
12.15	Interview 3
1.00	Assess Candidate 3
1.15	Lunch
2.00	Prepare Interview 4
2.15	Interview 4
3.00	Assess Candidate 4
3.15	Prepare Interview 5
3.30	Interview 5
4.15	Assess Candidate 5
4.30	Review interviews, select successful candidate, and complete paperwork
5.00	Close

Appendix 7

Interview Plan

Lead Responsibility	Time Allowed	Criteria to Cover	Note Taker
Chairperson	10 minutes	Welcome and Introductions Opening strength-based question Criteria 1—Relevant knowledge and experience	Member A
Member A	10–15 minutes	Criteria 2—Customer Relations Criteria 3—Communicating Effectively	Member B
Member B	10–15 minutes	Criteria 4—People Management Skills Criteria 5—Task Management	Member A
Chairperson	10 minutes	Criteria 6—Financial Awareness Any outstanding questions Close the interview	Member B

Appendix 8

Interview Preparation Sheet

Complete a separate interview preparation sheet for each of the criteria you are testing.

Criteria:	
Opening Question	Notes
Possible Follow-up Questions	

Appendix 9

Interview Record Sheet

Prepare a separate interview record sheet for each of the criteria you are testing.

Criteria:-	
Opening Question	**Notes**
Possible Follow-up Questions	

Appendix 10

Interview Rating List

	Candidate Name	Score
1		
2		
3		
4		
5		

Signed...

Chair:

Member A:

Member B:

Date:

Bibliography

Books

Hampden-Turner, C., and F. Trompenaars. 2001. *Riding the Waves of Culture: Understanding Cultural Diversity in Business.* Nicholas Brealey.

Rowntree, D. 1999. *The Manager's Book of Checklists: Instant Management Solutions When you Need Them.* Pitman Publishing.

Shepherd, E. 2008. *Investigative Interviewing: The Conversation Management Approach.* Oxford University Press, USA.

Whiddett, S., and S. Hollyforde. 2003. *A Practical Guide to Competencies: How to Enhance Individual and Organisational Performance.* CIPD Publishing.

Articles

Baska, M. February 2019. "What's Your Job Ad Really Saying?" People Management Magazine.

Brittain, S. "Interviewing Skills: Building a Solid Structure." peoplemanagement.co.uk

Burt, E.L. February 2019. "Stop Getting Hiring Wrong." People Management Magazine.

Fernández-Aráoz, C., B. Groysberg, and N. Nohria. 2009. "The Definitive Guide to Recruiting in Good Times and Bad." *Harvard Business Review* 87, no. 5, pp. 74–84.

Fernandez-Araoz, C. 1999. "Hiring Without Firing." *Harvard Business Review* 77, pp. 108–121.

Lewis. G. "Forget Everything You Know About Recruitment" peoplemanagement.co.uk

Makoff-Clark, A. 2019. "Is This The Secret to the Perfect Hire?" People Management Magazine

O'Leary, M. 2015. "Why Does Recruitment Fail?" *Employer Guides*, October 2015.

Reade, Q. "Employers Stick to Gut Reaction During Interview Process" www.personneltoday.com

Simpson, L. "Best Behaviour." www.personneltoday.com

Unattributed. "Behavior Description Technologies." *What is BD?*, www.bdt.net

About the Author

Stephen Amos MSc, is a training consultant and author. He has worked with a wide range of clients, including government departments, multinational corporations and small businesses. His specialisms include recruitment and selection interviewing. As a manager with the UK Civil Service he sat on numerous selection panels, and he has built on this experience to help many clients develop their ability to conduct successful recruitment campaigns.

Stephen has an MSc in Training and Performance Management. His dissertation was on the application of competency frameworks, including their use in recruitment and selection.

Index

OTHER TITLES IN THE HUMAN RESOURCE MANAGEMENT AND ORGANIZATIONAL BEHAVIOR COLLECTION

- *The Generation Myth* by Michael J. Urick
- *Practicing Leadership* by Alan S. Gutterman
- *Women Leaders* by Sapna Welsh
- *Untenable* by Gary Covert
- *The Relevance of Humanities to the 21st Century Workplace* by Michael Edmondson
- *Uniquely Great* by Lucy English

Announcing the Business Expert Press Digital Library

Concise e-books business students need for classroom and research

This book can also be purchased in an e-book collection by your library as

- a one-time purchase,
- that is owned forever,
- allows for simultaneous readers,
- has no restrictions on printing, and
- can be downloaded as PDFs from within the library community.

Our digital library collections are a great solution to beat the rising cost of textbooks. E-books can be loaded into their course management systems or onto students' e-book readers.
The **Business Expert Press** digital libraries are very affordable, with no obligation to buy in future years. For more information, please visit **www.businessexpertpress.com/librarians**. To set up a trial in the United States, please email **sales@businessexpertpress.com**.

www.ingramcontent.com/pod-product-compliance
Lightning Source LLC
Chambersburg PA
CBHW061310220326
41599CB00026B/4816